R. P

BROKER OF DEATH

BROKER OF DEATH

*An Insider's Story of
the Iranian Arms Deals*

Hermann Moll

with Michael Leapman

**MACMILLAN
LONDON**

First published 1988 by
MACMILLAN LONDON LIMITED
4 Little Essex Street London WC2R 3LF
and Basingstoke

Associated companies in Auckland, Delhi, Dublin, Gaborone,
Hamburg, Harare, Hong Kong, Johannesburg, Kuala Lumpur,
Lagos, Manzini, Melbourne, Mexico City, Nairobi, New York,
Singapore and Tokyo

British Library Cataloguing in Publication Data

Moll, Hermann
Broker of death: an insider's story of the Iranian arms deals.
1. Munitions
I. Title   II. Leapman, Michael
382′.456234′0924   HD9743.A2
ISBN 0-333-45942-3

Typeset by Columns of Reading
Printed and bound in Hong Kong

Contents

Cast of Main Characters

Bar-Am, Avraham: Retired Israeli general who carried a letter authorising him to act in the sale of Israeli military equipment. He was in the Israeli group arrested with Sam Evans in Bermuda. He claimed that he could, if he wanted, implicate senior Israeli officials in the scheme: but he stayed silent.

Bihn, Hans: Fellow defendant. German shipowner connected with Nicos Minardos, he recruited Kopka to the enterprise. He was arrested in New York a day later than the rest of us. I stayed with him in Connecticut immediately after my release.

Brenneke, Richard: Well-connected Oregon businessman, associate of de la Rocque, who sought to inform senior White House officials, including Vice-President Bush, about the Evans/Hashemi deal, but aroused little interest.

Bush, George: Vice-President of the USA and former head of the Central Intelligence Agency. How much he knew about the Iran/Contra affair has never been established, but if Veillot's and de la Rocque's account is to be believed he was in the thick of it.

Casey, William: Director of the Central Intelligence Agency from 1981 until his resignation in February 1987. Died the following May. Old friend of Roy Furmark, the man who introduced Sam Evans to Cyrus Hashemi.

de la Rocque, John: Mystery figure who, with Bernard Veillot, claimed to have access to large quantities of US arms. He was telling Sam Evans about the Irangate deals long before they were revealed publicly, so he clearly had good links with the administration. Possibly a CIA agent.

Doyle, Dennis: US customs agent, working under Joe King, who played an active role in my entrapment and arrest.

Eisenberg, Israel and Guri: Fellow defendants. Israeli insurance brokers who were among the group arrested in Bermuda on 22 April 1986.

Evans, Samuel: Fellow defendant. American lawyer based in London who got me involved in the enterprise when he introduced me to Hashemi. Arrested in Bermuda the day after I was arrested in New York and, like me, is on bail awaiting trial. Lawyer for Adnan Kashoggi.

Flearmoy, Albert: Fellow defendant. An Englishman in his sixties who owned a hairdressing chain and had done some arms deals with Rhodesia when Britain was imposing sanctions. Arrested with Kopka a few hours before me.

Furmark, Roy: New York businessman, former client of Sam Evans, who helped set our deal in motion by introducing Sam to Hashemi. Through Sam, he built a relationship with Adnan Kashoggi and through him was involved in the North deals. An old friend of the late William Casey, director of the CIA, Furmark provides one of the strong links between our case and the Iran/Contra affair.

Ghorbanifar, Manuchehr: Arms dealer who acted as link man with the Iranians in Colonel North's Iran/Contra deals. Met Sam Evans in Hamburg in June 1985.

Giuliani, Rudolph: District Attorney for the southern district of New York who helped organise the sting and whose office is prosecuting the case. Politically ambitious, he thought it to his advantage to go through with the case even after the Irangate revelations seemed to have removed most of the foundation of it.

Hashemi, Cyrus: Banker and arms dealer, cousin of Speaker of Iranian Parliament. Central figure in the sting that trapped me and sixteen others. Had played a role in attempts to free the US hostages held in Iran in 1980. Died mysteriously in London in July 1986.

Hashemi, Mohammed Ali (Jamshid): London-based brother of Cyrus and former partner in arms deals. Indicted in New York with Cyrus in 1984. Believes strongly that Cyrus was murdered.

Kashoggi, Adnan: Saudi arms dealer and entrepreneur, once a billionaire but reportedly in recent financial difficulties. Financed the North/Ghorbanifar arms-for-hostages deals.

Kimche, David: Former Director-General of Israel's Foreign Ministry who encouraged the arms deals being negotiated by Sam Evans as well as by North.

King, Joe: US customs agent in New York who helped organise the sting and who posed as a colleague of Hashemi at some of the meetings with Sam Evans and the others.

Kopka, Ralph: Fellow defendant. A German businessman recruited to the deal by Flearmoy, with whom he was arrested in New York on 21 April 1986.

Lavi, Houshang: Iranian-born CIA agent. He played a walk-on role in the sting operation and claims to have been told by Joe King, an agent for the US customs in New York, that 'we' had disposed of Hashemi by killing him.

McFarlane, Robert: National Security Adviser to President Reagan from October 1983 to November 1985. He approved

North's initial approaches to Iran and went on a secret mission to Tehran in May 1986 to pursue discussions on arms-for-hostages swap.

Meese, Edwin, III: As Attorney-General he carried ultimate responsibility for all federal prosecutions such as ours, as well as for the sting that led up to it. He was also kept informed of Oliver North's deals – so he knew we were being charged under a law that was being flouted in the White House, although he denied any knowledge of such deals when asked by the judge.

Minardos, Nicos: Fellow defendant. US citizen, born in Greece and living in California, part-time actor and wheeler-dealer who knew Sam Evans through having done business with Kashoggi.

North, Lieutenant-Colonel Oliver: When on the National Security Commission, was the chief operating officer on the Iran/Contra deals. Dismissed from NSC when details were revealed in November 1986.

Northrop, William: Fellow defendant. American living in Israel who claimed to be a member of the Northrop aviation family. One of the Israeli group arrested in Bermuda with Sam Evans on 22 April 1986.

Poindexter, Rear-Admiral John: Succeeded McFarlane as National Security Adviser to President Reagan in December 1985. Authorised and approved the Iran/Contra deals. Resigned in November 1986.

Rafsanjani, Hashemi: Speaker of the Iranian Parliament – one of the most powerful offices in the land. Cousin of Cyrus Hashemi.

Reagan, Ronald: President of the United States, 1981 to 1988, former film actor who approved Oliver North's arms-for-hostages deals with Iran.

Rowland, 'Tiny': Chairman of multinational corporation Lonrho. Approached by Kashoggi to provide funds for the North/Ghorbanifar deals.

Sand, Leonard: The federal judge presiding over our case.

Schofield, Lorna: Assistant US attorney responsible for prosecuting our case on a day-to-day basis.

Shultz, George: Reagan's Secretary of State. He knew of the arms-for-hostages deals in outline but persistently advised against them.

Veillot, Bernard: Partner of de la Rocque who, through Sam, offered Hashemi thirty-nine F–4Es for direct delivery from the United States. A CIA agent who had good information about secret US policy towards Iran.

von Raab, William: US customs service Commissioner, whose office organised the sting and who coined the phrase 'brokers of death' to describe the defendants on the day after our arrest.

Weinberger, Caspar: Secretary for Defense. Like Shultz, he was opposed to North's Iran/Contra deals. Resigned November 1987.

1

Set-up on First Avenue

New York seemed all right so far, although after only three hours it was maybe too early to judge. This was my first time there and I had not, in all honesty, wanted to go. But I couldn't help being turned on by the night-time view from my window table at the Top of the Tower bar, on the penthouse floor of the Beekman Tower Hotel on First Avenue. It was just like you see in the movies and on TV. To my right was a jumble of tall buildings stretching towards a strip of glowing lights: that, I supposed, was Broadway and the entertainment district. It was a shame that my tight schedule would not give me time to sample that, because ever since I was a teenager in Germany I have been a bit of an expert on girly bars and the pleasures that go with them; but I had to get back to my adopted home in London by the following night's plane. There was important business to finish and, besides, my girlfriend Noi was expecting me. Next time, maybe I'd be able to spend a bit longer here.

Ahead of me rose the clean lines of the brightly lit skyscraper that housed the United Nations, the symbol of man's well-intentioned attempt to make peace and justice prevail in the world. There was no sign of it succeeding – luckily for me in a way, because if it did I would be out of business. It was funny, I thought, that such an idealistic institution should be located in a city with so corrupt a reputation. Indeed the lawless aspect of New York's life had a lot to do with my being there, alone at a table by the window, sipping my first gin-and-tonic for several hours, at around 10.15 p.m. on Monday, 21 April 1986. And it led directly to what happened next.

Normally, I love travelling to new places, especially to big cities: the bigger the better. It was one of the many attractions of the business that I had been engaged in for four years and at which I was just beginning to gain an international reputation – and, most important, to make serious sums of money. I am a freelance supplier of military equipment, or what is popularly known as an arms dealer. I had been persuaded to fly to New York for one night, although it was an inconvenient time, to sew up a deal that had been simmering away for nearly six months. It would be the biggest pay day of my twenty-nine-year life. The deal involved planes, tanks and missiles worth a total of $320 million. The customer, as with many of the largest arms transactions of the 1980s, was Iran, which had found it difficult to obtain arms by conventional means since the Ayatollah Khomeini's revolution had ousted the Shah in January 1979. I had been dealing with a faintly mysterious Iranian banker named Cyrus Hashemi, a cousin of Hashemi Rafsanjani, the Speaker in the Iranian Parliament. We had been introduced by Sam Evans, a well-connected American lawyer I knew in London, who numbered among his clients the celebrated international businessman Adnan Kashoggi.

Cyrus Hashemi was also based in London and normally I would not have expected to be required to go to New York to clinch the deal. But there had been problems in prising out of him the first down-payment for the package. There was nothing particularly unusual about that. I have lost count of the number of deals I have started that broke down when the time came for the customer to pay up. Anyone will tell you that it's one of the hazards of this business. If you complete more than a tenth of the deals you start, then you're ahead of the game. But you have to pursue them all up to that point, because you can never tell which one out of the ten will go through. It's like trying to lay a seductive but unavailable woman. She's all smiles and sexiness as she leads you on at the beginning, and then she suddenly switches off when the time comes to get her into the sack. When the deals do come off – just like when the woman comes across – it's a tremendous feeling.

There had been some odd things about this transaction from the start. The first was that Hashemi was only interested in American equipment. There didn't seem any logical reason for that. It was true that the Iranian army had normally used American equipment in the past – a legacy of the deposed Shah's close relationship with the United States – but it was perverse to insist on them now, especially when America had imposed an embargo on arms trade with Iran, accusing the revolutionary regime of being involved in international terrorism. Although I knew – as the world would know later – that the embargo was being flouted by the US government itself, it still made things difficult for the Iranians on the international arms market. They could hardly afford to be choosy.

Hashemi said $500 million had been earmarked for American material and was held at the Chemical Bank in New York. But I had never been able to get any proper proof that the funds existed. The normal thing in this business would be for the customer's bank to send a telex to my bank – the Banque Bruxelles Lambert in Brussels – confirming that adequate funds are held in a particular account. But Chemical had never done that. There had been a phone call to Brussels from a top man at Chemical, but phone calls do not satisfy bankers. They want something on paper. Hashemi had made dozens of phone calls to me and said that if I visited New York to sign the deal he could let me have $115,000 in cash and a letter of credit for $1½ million. That was a powerful attraction after the months of frustration.

But another worrying thing was that I had done some investigating and found that Hashemi's brother had been in trouble with the police in America. (So had Hashemi but I did not know that then.) Was the Iranian being used by the US authorities as a bait to trap me? I'd read of such things but it didn't seem to make sense. Sam Evans had assured me that Hashemi was reliable. Once I remarked to him, 'This guy seems a little strange,' but Sam had replied, 'That's the way he is. I've known him for a few years and he's legit.'

In any case, I was certain that this deal had the official sanction of the White House, though by the nature of things that would never be announced publicly. And anyway, why should anyone want to frame me? I'd had very few dealings with Americans in the past, which was why I hadn't been to the States before. All the same, I had been drinking with an Arab friend in London a couple of days earlier and told him, 'I have a funny gut feeling about this trip.' And I did not decide finally to go until after lunch on the day of the flight. In the following months, how I wished that my doubts had prevailed.

I packed a shoulder bag with all I needed for one night away – a sponge bag, some night things and a change of shirt – then drove to the newly opened Terminal 4 at Heathrow and caught the last jumbo of the day, British Airways flight 179, which leaves at 6.30 in the evening. I settled into my first-class seat, ordered the first of several gin-and-tonics and dozed off during the movie. At 8.30 New York time I was walking through US immigration at JFK airport and telling the officer there that I was an advertising salesman – which was partly true. Outside the customs hall I saw a youngish man waiting with my name scrawled on a piece of board. He introduced himself as Hashemi's driver and took me to a Mercedes 500 SEL for the half-hour drive into Manhattan. We passed through the long tunnel under the East River, then headed north up First Avenue. The driver pointed out the UN building to me just before we turned right up a slight slope and pulled up in front of the entrance to the Beekman Tower.

The driver already had the key and we went straight up in the lift into the suite that had been reserved for me on the fourteenth floor. It was large and comfortable but a bit tatty. The furnishings were the sort of reproduction antiques you see in any classy American hotel, but they looked the worse for wear, and so did the wallpaper. The driver said Hashemi would ring me in half an hour. I washed and shaved and felt a bit better: I always drink too much gin on planes. Hashemi duly called and invited me to his suite, just below mine on the thirteenth floor. As I waited for the lift I remembered I'd been told that the Americans, for superstitious reasons, didn't usually have a thirteenth floor in their hotels. As I always say, never believe anything people tell you.

In the suite, almost identical to mine, we spoke for a bit more than half an hour. As I sat in the bar cradling my drink and looking across the skyline, I thought back over the conversation and was reassured. Hashemi had confirmed that I would pick up the money and the letter of credit the following day, when I would also meet a key associate who worked at the Iranian mission to the UN: that was why he had chosen this hotel for us, right next to the UN building. I wondered slightly whether I had shot my mouth off a bit during the meeting. My friends say I do that when I've had a few to drink, but I tell them I'm a salesman and part of the job is to convince people that you've been around and that there's nothing that you can't perform for them. In any case, it was past two in the morning by London time, and it had been a tiring flight.

Hashemi had seemed specially interested in two things – the origin of the arms I was selling him and the mechanics of getting a false end-user certificate (EUC) for them. He still insisted that the weapons had to be American, although I kept telling him that other countries, such as Austria and Germany, made stuff just as good. The EUC is something all major governments require, to ensure that their arms do not go to countries they disapprove of. Despite the embargo, Sam Evans and others involved in the deal believed it was certain that the Americans approved sales of their arms to Iran. The Israelis were known to be selling the Iranians equipment which they had bought from the United States and the Americans were in turn re-equipping the Israelis. We also suspected that more direct supplies were being made. But if the Americans would still not formally approve arms sales to Iran, it would mean getting a false EUC showing that the supplies were going somewhere else.

I had tried all along to give Hashemi the idea that a false EUC would be no problem, although expensive. Had we really been trying to dupe the Americans it would certainly have been harder than I had suggested but, I repeat, I am a salesman. I spoke as though it was the kind of thing I did every working day and perhaps I should have been more cautious. But the truth was that if the Americans were genuinely trying to prevent arms being sold in the quantities we were talking about, they would have investigated the deal thoroughly and no false EUC in the world would have got past them. I know they are not stupid and nor am I. Only if they were content to let us go ahead – as I thought they were – would they turn a blind eye to an attempt to deceive them.

Quite aside from that, it may have been over-bold of me to tell Hashemi about my earlier suspicions that he was setting me up for the authorities.

'Let me be very honest with you,' I told him. 'I was at one time a bit suspicious. Am I right when I say that your brother is in . . . is in the United States and in trouble?'

Hashemi looked at me hard and replied quietly, 'Yes.'

'Yes,' I echoed him. 'And the idea which came to me was that . . . well, that the CIA might put some pressure on you in order to get information or whatever. And I wasn't very sure about this trip, not very sure about coming here.'

He seemed unmoved. 'Yes,' he said again simply.

It was a bit unnerving but I continued, trying to ease the tension, 'But I would say that, if that had been the case, I would not be sitting here now.'

Hashemi threw his head back and laughed quickly. 'I have no contact with CIA,' he assured me. 'None whatsoever.'

I laughed with him and said, 'I don't want any. I don't want any at all. You know, I try to keep away from these boys . . . I don't feel like going on a state pension.'

I had been reassured by his denial, although, looking back on the conversation as I took my first sip of gin in the bar, I recognised that this was the response he would have had to give, whatever the truth of my suggestion. I had relaxed after that edgy exchange and we had gone on to discuss the possibility of new deals beyond the one I had gone to clinch. In truth it was not much of a discussion. I was doing most of the talking and Hashemi just primed me with a few questions and interruptions. Perhaps I got a bit carried away at one point, when I suggested that I might fly some of the equipment to Tehran myself, in a light plane from Dubai, and that he could arrange a code so that the control tower at Tehran airport would know they must give me landing permission. He had smiled comfortingly and indicated that this could be arranged without difficulty.

There was another bit of conversation that I now remembered, which went right to the heart of the arms business and my attitude to it. I had raised the possibility of selling Hashemi some Microlite aircraft. These are small, inexpensive, flexible, heavily armoured planes, operated by one person, capable of doing enormous damage, although somewhat vulnerable to attack.

'If you lose one,' I had told him, 'okay, you lose one pilot and one plane. You lost a life. Well, in a war, one life . . . every day you lose thousands. But as a country you cannot look at only one soldier. As a country, you have to look at the cost. War is the most expensive hobby; a most expensive business, for sure.'

We had ended the talk by agreeing to meet at around ten the next morning. 'It's three in the morning in London now, so I'm waking up again,' I told Hashemi. He smiled. I took the lift to the ground floor to search for the bar, but they told me it was right at the top of the building, so I took the special express lift up again. It was an elaborate cocktail bar, decorated in black and silver, with lots of stainless steel and marble. Its high vaulted roof made it feel something like a Gothic cathedral: rather too cold and unfriendly for the kind of companionable drinking places I feel most at home in. But the view was undeniably romantic and there was no shortage of customers.

The waiters wore formal dress and one led me to a table by the window. 'They know how to serve drinks here, anyway,' I thought, as I took my first sip of the stiff gin-and-tonic, in a tall glass crammed with ice and a large slice of lemon. Looking back over the meeting with Hashemi I was fairly satisfied. It was true I had not yet actually laid hands on any money but it wasn't conceivable, surely, that he would bring me all this way if he didn't mean business. And he had seemed quite interested in the additional items I had proposed to him. There could be a great deal of money indeed in our quiet friend Cyrus Hashemi . . .

My train of thought was interrupted by a disturbance behind me, a jumble of rapid footsteps that I couldn't instantly identify. Before I could turn round I felt something cold on the back of my neck. My instant reaction was that a waiter must have spilled a drink on me but in less than a second I realised that what I felt was metal being pressed hard against my flesh.

'Don't make any move. US Federal Customs. Mr Hermann Moll, you are under arrest.'

Twelve customs agents surrounded me, six of them pointing revolvers at my face. Although my mind was in a turmoil, I instantly identified the guns as Smith and Wesson .38 specials. In my business you recognise firearms as fast as you recognise people. I was scarcely listening as a member of the group, with a distinctively pock-marked face, said something about a conspiracy and read me my rights, just like the TV cops do: 'You have the right to remain silent . . .'

I was pulled out of my chair, flung against the wall and made to spread my legs and arms. My instinct was to look for a way of escape but a moment's thought persuaded me that was unrealistic. All conversation in the bar had ended as the other drinkers watched with uncomprehending fascination. Like me, some had probably arrived in New York only that evening. A few may never have been to the city before. It was living up to its image with a vengeance. Maybe some of them thought we were shooting a movie. In fact, it was all too real.

I recognised one of my assailants. He was the young man who had met me two hours earlier at JFK airport. When I saw him standing close to me in the bar, his eyes glistening in triumph, I understood what had happened. My suspicions about Hashemi, the fears I had been discussing lightly with him just half an hour ago, had been absolutely spot on. I had been set up.

The customs agents handcuffed me and accompanied me to my suite, searched my overnight bag and told me I would

be driven downtown to the customs house at the World
Trade Center. As we left the hotel and I was pushed into a
police car, I saw that the side street leading to it had been
cordoned off. Just what did they think I was planning to do?
Make a dash for it? When I had six armed men all round
me? It all seemed like a dream. What was I being accused
of? What did they mean about a conspiracy? I guessed that
they had been listening in to my conversation with Hashemi
but I didn't think boasting was a criminal act, even in
America.

There had been one woman in the team who arrested me
and she seemed to be in charge. When we reached the
Customs House she again read me my rights. By now I had
decided that I would not say anything until I had obtained a
lawyer. They refused to let me make a phone call. Then for
the first time I came face to face with another young woman,
who would be my main adversary in the months ahead. Her
name was Lorna Schofield, and she was an assistant in the
United States attorney's office in New York, and she was to
be the prosecuting counsel in my case. Schofield must have
been her married name because she was clearly of Filipino
extraction.

She tried to charm me at first. I do not usually resist
female advances and I have always regarded Asian women
as my type. But although I was still confused and bewildered
as to what exactly was happening, it was obviously a serious
business that could not be mixed with pleasure. When I
would not yield to her and still refused to say anything, she
warned me that I faced eighty-five years in prison. They put
me into a large cell in the Metropolitan Correction Center
(MCC for short), New York's top-security jail. There was no
bed. I asked for water but did not get any.

My planned overnight stay in New York was to extend to
ten and a half months. Before I left, my case would become
world famous because of its links with the scandal that
threatened to destroy the Reagan presidency just as Water-
gate had destroyed President Nixon. In the ensuing weeks I
had plenty of time to reconstruct in my mind exactly how it
had all happened and how I had become involved. But for

the moment, quite irrationally, a single thought entered my head and nagged at me even more than my present predicament. I remembered I had left my car, my precious Jaguar XK 120, in the short-term car park at Terminal 4. It was clocking up charges at the rate of £15.60 a day.

2

The Trail from Park Lane

Looking back to how it all began, the place to start is Les Ambassadeurs, London's most opulent and ostentatious club. It occupies an expensively decorated nineteenth-century mansion at the southern end of Park Lane that once belonged to the Rothschilds, the millionaire bankers. That part of London is now a favourite haunt of wealthy Arabs, and the club caters to them, as well as to the financiers and dealers of various kinds who do business with them. The food is of the highest international standard and the wine list has bottles priced at up to £350. In short, it is the sort of club I dreamed of being able to afford to join when I set out to be an arms dealer. Conversations in the restaurant and bar are usually furtive, as though shady deals are possibly being transacted – but the club's credentials are perfectly respectable. On a board near the entrance Lord Havers, the former Attorney-General and Lord Chancellor, is listed as being on the committee.

I had belonged to Les Ambassadeurs since 1984, soon after I began dealing in arms. My then partner, John Saunders, had proposed my membership. It was, he said, a useful place to meet the kind of people who might one day be our customers. One evening in 1984 Robert Mills, chairman of the club and the man who basically runs it, suggested I might like to meet another of his members, the American lawyer Sam Evans. Mills sees it as part of his job to ease contacts between members with mutual interests. It is one of the benefits of club membership, profitable to all concerned.

Sam is an American business lawyer with an English wife.

He has practised in London for twenty years. Tall, slim and in his forties, with sleek grey hair, he looks like an aristocrat and comes from a wealthy landed family in St Louis. He used to work for J. Paul Getty, the oil millionaire. Sam has an expensive town house in Chester Square, the most exclusive address in the well-heeled London district of Belgravia, furnished in the best of taste. His office is not far away in Grosvenor Place, close to Hyde Park Corner.

At Mills' suggestion, I phoned Evans at Grosvenor Place. He said he had just helped establish a company called Curzon Merchants, which was going into the arms business. The main figure in the new company was Mel Thompson, an American, and Sam said the best way to start would be for me to meet Thompson for a talk. With my partner John Saunders, we got together that evening for a drink at Les A. Thompson was in his forties, short – no more than five foot seven – with a stocky build and glasses. He reminded me a bit of the characters who play CIA agents in American movies: even his hair was cropped to a military length. He had brought with him his blonde and attractive secretary.

He said he was looking to do arms deals with a variety of countries. He did not at that stage mention Iran specifically, but I knew that this was where a lot of privately bought weapons were going at that time. I also knew that Kashoggi was involved in the Iranian deals and that Evans worked for Kashoggi. Thompson asked me to get him as many quotations as possible for what was available, so that they could look round the market to see if they could sell it. We talked for around an hour. I promised I would get the quotations and we would see where it led from there.

Next day, at my office in Cricklewood, I got my secretary to type out a list of items I could secure. They included: 50,000 rounds of 155mm HE (high explosive) shells, made in Greece; communication and night-vision equipment; 200 Browning machine guns, refurbished in England. I could have given him a much fuller list but, because Curzon Merchants was a new company with no track record, I had doubts about whether the deal would come off. I did not think it worthwhile to make strenuous efforts to locate supplies. I also had reservations, confirmed later, about Thompson's qualifications in the arms trade. He did not say anything about his background – in this business people seldom do. On the other hand I did know who Sam was. The Kashoggi connection meant that there might, after all, be something in it.

I met Sam for the first time at the offices of Curzon Merchants a couple of weeks later. They were in a ground floor and basement in Curzon Street, on the left as you walk down from Park Lane. It was a small but comfortable office, with a large desk and deeply upholstered settee. Mel was waiting when I arrived and Sam turned up in a few minutes, as we were sitting on the settee drinking coffee. When we started talking I realised that Sam did not have a lot of product knowledge but was better at the contractual side. He asked me naive questions such as 'What does HE stand for?' He said Kashoggi was in no way involved in the venture and that the work he did for the Saudi did not include arms transactions. I guessed that, having seen from Kashoggi how much money could be made in the business, he wanted to get into it on his own account – although he was rich enough by most standards. He might also have wanted a second string to his bow, given the rumours then current about Kashoggi's financial situation.

I gave him a short rundown on the goods I was offering and on this occasion Iran was mentioned. Everyone in the arms business at that time was talking about Israel selling arms to Iran with American knowledge, and the Americans supplying Israel with arms to replace them. It was officially denied but later it all came out. When we heard President Reagan on television agonising about the Iranians being terrorists it made me laugh, because everyone was aware what his government was up to. The Israelis were even selling back to Iran arms that had been captured from them by the Iraqis, and which they had obtained through independent channels.

Israel's motives were quite clear. Two of their enemies were going at each other's throats. They thought it in their interests to provide Iran with weapons to kill Iraqis. The

American thinking was much the same, but with an added element: Iraq was friendly with the Soviet Union, and if the Iraqis won the war it would mean an expansion of Russian influence in the Middle East.

I was in fact already working on a deal with Iran through an Iranian named Razabi based in Kensington, who was interested in basically the same products I offered Curzon Merchants. You need to have as many feelers as possible out at any one time. There are so many people in this business who tell you, 'I've got the right contacts, I know the right people,' that you take it with a pinch of salt.

That is especially true in the case of Iran. Until September 1987, when the British government closed it down, the Iranians had their famous arms-purchasing office in Victoria Street, but they did not buy equipment exclusively from there. In addition, there are quite a few people running round the world with letters in their pockets who are looking for arms for Iran. They approach dealers like me and say they have brothers or cousins in the Iranian government or with good connections to it, and that they have authority to do any deals. Razabi was a typical example. His brother was in Iran and his cousin was on some sort of arms-procurement committee. Since the Shah's days Iran has not changed a lot. There is still this commission game going on and people like to make backhanders. More often than not, though, the deals never happen. With Razabi I gave him a quotation and dozens of telexes went back and forth to Tehran. We did do a deal in the end, but much smaller than the one we were talking about to begin with.

Sam Evans was different. His background gave his words more weight than the others. He was a thoughtful man. We had a discussion about the hypocrisy of President Reagan in denouncing the Iranians as devils while allowing them to be supplied with American arms. We also talked about German equipment, which has a great reputation for quality and which I know a lot about. But you always run into the same problem there. Everybody wants to buy things such as the Leopard 1 and Leopard 2 tanks but the company that makes them never gets permission from the government to sell them to Arab countries. It's the result of the Holocaust, which is still on Germany's conscience. The Germans wouldn't want to run the risk of German equipment being used against Israel.

In fact the German government is very sensitive about its weapons being used on any battlefield. It doesn't make much sense, because German submarines are sold to Chile and tactically they're extremely valuable weapons, carrying electronic equipment and missiles that could kill hundreds of thousands of people. But the government won't allow sub-machine guns to be sold to the same country. They're frightened that if there was a student demonstration in Santiago the police would mow down the students with Heckler and Koch guns, which would be seen on television screens all over the world. It's frustrating for the German companies when they can't get export licences. But the customers get the guns in the end because firms like Heckler and Koch sell manufacturing plants to Latin American countries which don't impose the same controls on sales.

Occasionally German weapons might be sold on to third countries by the original buyers. There is nothing the German authorities can do about that. Sometimes, too, the controls are skirted by acquiring false end-user certificates, but that is not easy. There are only a few countries that Germany is sufficiently friendly with to approve the sales of arms, and you cannot bribe the entire defence ministries of those countries. Small, corrupt countries, where you can buy the defence minister himself, are unlikely to be on the German government's approved list.

Evans, Thompson and I spoke about these matters for about an hour, and they seemed impressed by the depth of my knowledge. I left my quotations with them and said, 'The ball is in your court. Let me know what you can do. I hope we can soon sit down and get a couple of deals going.'

Things progressed slowly. Thompson gave me intermittent progress reports and a few weeks later asked me for a quote for more communications equipment – 500 field telephones. I got a quotation from Racal but then found out that the same company was in Iran trying to do the same deal direct with the government. They had the problem everyone else had in Iran, of not knowing whether their man had as good a line of contact with the authorities as he said he had. The sensible dealer works through several different agents at the same time. In the end, as in so many cases, nothing came of those Iranian deals with Curzon Merchants. But I sensed that in the urbane Sam Evans I had made possibly my most significant contact in my brief career in the arms game. Just how significant, and in what way, I was not yet to know. For that day a business relationship was established which would guide me into the farrago of lies and deception that, nearly three years later, the world came to know as Irangate.

I was born in Cologne on 22 September 1956. My parents were middle class: my father a mechanic fixing machinery in a factory making clay pipes, while my mother stayed at home to look after me and my elder brother and sister. We lived in a decent flat and had a car. My brother has lost contact with us now, and my sister is a housewife.

I went to school in a small town called Frechen, eight miles south of the city. In Germany you go to school for nine years and then either leave and get a job or go to another school and pass your matriculation, the equivalent of A levels in Britain. I did that but left school at seventeen and didn't go to university. From the age of fourteen I started earning my own money as an usher in a cinema. That was when I had my first woman, a twenty-five-year-old hooker I met in a bar. She was the sister of a friend of mine and she didn't charge me for the favour. It was a one-night stand, but it made me realise I was attractive to women and from then I began hunting them seriously. My life fell into a pattern: I would go to school in the mornings, make money in the evenings and chase women at weekends.

I used to read a lot of books, especially about travel. From my very earliest years I had one thing clear in my mind: I did not want to be middle class for the rest of my days. I did not want the sort of unexciting, mundane life my parents lived, working from eight till five with only Sunday off, doing overtime so that we could afford a holiday in Italy once a year. It was clear to me from the age of fourteen that this life was not for me, which was why I read travel books to feed my imagination. There was a whole world out there waiting to be discovered.

I am six foot two inches tall and was already big at fourteen – I would be taken for sixteen or eighteen and my friends were all between eighteen and twenty-two, boys as well as girls. People of my own age seemed to me childish and had different interests. I would spend my money on going out and trying to pick up women, with increasing success. I also saved a bit. I had a simple objective – to get rich – but no idea how I was going to achieve it. My parents used to say it was better to be poor and healthy than rich and sick. I would reply that it was better to be rich and healthy.

At fourteen, too, another critical event in my life occurred, when I went to London for the first time, with a school group. I looked around and told myself: 'This is my city, *the* city.' I vowed that one day I would live and work there. With Berlin divided, Germany has no city of its size or excitement. It is four times as big as Cologne and I realised that there was an awful lot of money there. There is a saying that if you want to make money you have to be where the money is. The world is ruled by it. Money, fast cars and beautiful women are symbols of success everywhere. That was the lifestyle for me. I wanted my share, and more.

When I left school I looked at ways of making big money fast. I had always been a good salesman, with the ability to talk well and persuade people. I knew several wealthy salesmen – and an equal number of poor professors. I decided that selling would be the best way for me to make a lot of money. To gain some experience I began working in a furniture shop in Cologne. My boss used to say that selling was not something you could learn, but was a talent you either had or hadn't. Obviously I had it because I was very successful.

But I knew lots of people of fifty who had worked very hard for other people all their lives without getting rich. I knew that if I wanted to make serious money I would have to work for myself. When I was nineteen I saw an ad for a salesman of office copying machines and word processors for the big office equipment firm of Pelikan. So I left the furniture company and joined them – my first step up. They gave me an Audi car, a great improvement on the Volkswagen I had driven before.

After eight months I was conscripted for national service in the army. I was furious because I was earning about $2400 a month – big money in those days. In the German army you get about $120 a month and you have to stay for eighteen months. I decided to get out of it by fixing the medical test. I tried everything – drank two litres of coffee and smoked 100 cigarettes – but it didn't work. The examiners' attitude was: 'If you've got two legs, two arms and a head, you are fit.'

I joined an infantry regiment and was sent to a training camp in northern Germany. It was a total waste of time and money, especially money. My policy was to make as little effort as I could, and pass the time without any problems. Basic training was a pain in the neck. We had to get up at four in the morning and run around for most of the day. The orders we were given were totally illogical. Now I'm a great believer in logic, but the training handbook seemed to have been written for morons, with ludicrous instructions like: 'If a soldier is in the water and it reaches his chin, he has to start swimming.' I was not amused, in short.

After six weeks' basic training I was transferred to a supply battalion at Schwanewede, near Hamburg. For a lot of reasons, it was a stroke of luck. To begin with, I had the opportunity of getting a licence to drive a heavy goods vehicle (HGV), which I thought would be useful in outside life – plus a licence to drive a tank, which I thought would be less useful. I passed all the tests and was given responsibility for supplying petrol for the whole army camp. Naturally, this cut the cost of my own drives home to Cologne.

One day, towards the end of my eighteen months, I was watching a film and saw people jumping out of aeroplanes. I thought this would be a challenge and, since my motto in life is to aim to try everything, I volunteered for a parachute course. It was one of those decisions that you take quickly and then, when it is too late, you regret it deeply. I have never been so terrified in my life. The practice sessions, when you jump from a high tower, are deceptively easy. You soon get used to it and you are lulled into a false sense of safety.

Nothing in the world can prepare you for the horror of standing in an aeroplane with the door open, looking down at the ground 2000 feet away, with the nightmarish sound of the engines assaulting your ears and mind. You wonder what on earth can have possessed you actually to put yourself forward for the ordeal. You feel terribly sick, have an urgent need to go to the lavatory and wonder if it is possible even at that stage to get out of it. But it is too late for that: too late for anything. You stand by the door for a few seconds until you hear the dreaded word:

'Jump.'

Somehow you force your body to obey the command. You know you are entirely dependent on the machinery of the parachute working. It is an automatic release that operates four seconds after you leave the aircraft. That first time was the longest four seconds I have ever endured. According to our training, as we hurtled towards the ground we had to count up to four slowly, like this:

'One thousand,

'Two thousand,

'Three thousand,

'Four thousand.'

Then there was a jerk around my neck as if somebody had grabbed me from behind and was trying to throttle me. But that did not necessarily mean that all was well. It could have been that something had caught and the parachute had not opened properly. That is the point when you are supposed to look up above you. I did so with extreme trepidation. That parachute billowing safely above me was the finest sight I have ever seen in my life.

From that point it was possible to enjoy the experience. I

was now out of earshot of the aircraft engine and there was not a sound. It was like another world. The ground was still a long way off but it was coming up to meet me at a tolerable pace. There was a forest directly below me and I remembered what I had been taught about manoeuvring the 'chute. I pulled a tag to get my back to the wind so that it would blow me clear of the forest to the field beyond. I guessed I was travelling at about forty-five miles an hour. Then I pulled another tag to turn in the other direction, facing the wind, to slow me in readiness for touchdown.

At around 200 feet I put my legs together to brace for the landing. There was a final moment of panic as the ground seemed to rush at me faster and faster. I discovered later that I had been given a parachute of the wrong size for my weight, so I landed heavily, as if I had jumped from a nine-foot wall. But I wasn't hurt and I felt an enormous sense both of relief and, I confess, of superiority over most of my fellow men. I had done it, I had achieved something that most people never manage to do in their lifetime. More important, I had managed to overcome my own fear.

I looked up. I could just see the plane I had jumped from, circling in the sky. I smiled. I cannot remember a moment in my life when I felt happier to be alive or more pleased to be the person I was. I had proved something to my army colleagues and to myself. I felt terrific.

The main advantage of my time in the army, in the light of what happened later, was that it allowed me to familiarise myself with weapons. I was trained on a number of them – sub-machine guns, machine guns, pistols, rifles. One day I saw a magazine from a German publisher lying on a table in someone's office. It was a defence magazine called *Wehrtechnik*, all about weapons systems. I read in it about how arms were sold to various countries. I knew that there were arms dealers around but I had not until then known what was involved. To me the arms dealer was a shady figure, engaged in a deadly but exciting business – and a profitable one, too. I worked out that the guys who did the deals must be getting handsome commissions.

'Hang on, Hermann,' I thought to myself. 'You know you have the talent of an entrepreneur and the arms business is clearly very lucrative.' So I started collecting these magazines and reading the articles and the advertisements, to gain as much knowledge as possible of the market. Over a period I thought about it and began to devise a plan. Like any other business you need experience and knowledge of the products, the market, the suppliers and buyers and the sources of capital.

But my first priority on leaving the army in 1976 was to get married. I was only twenty – much too young really but I have always been impatient to get on with things. I had met Doreen, six years older than me, not long before I was called up and we had been seeing a lot of each other during my leave periods and at weekends. She was an Asian from Trinidad, working at a hospital at Freschen. I met her on a tram one Sunday when I was out chasing birds in Cologne. She spoke English – which fitted in with my plan to go to London. We used to speak only English at home, and gradually I became more fluent. Later the new EEC laws made it easier for a German to settle in England. Doreen and I steered away from children because I thought they would limit my flexibility in future.

I spent some time looking around the job market and doing a few short-term jobs. Then I saw an ad placed in a Cologne newspaper by Mönch, the publisher of the arms magazine that I had been so taken with. They are a biggish company, based in Bonn, and they were looking for a marketing man. I called them and applied. I don't believe in writing letters: I prefer the direct approach.

I spoke to the marketing director, Herr Helex, and arranged to go and see him. They were looking for a marketing man for Germany, Austria and Switzerland, concentrating particularly on selling advertising in a new publication, the NATO sixteen-nation defence-equipment catalogue. Mönch had been trying to market it for three years without success. The interview lasted about an hour. Helex asked the standard questions, like what I expected to put into the job and to get out of it; but the most important of them was: 'What sort of money had you in mind?'

When I told him my financial ideas, he shrank. I said I needed 5000 marks a month (about $3000). I added confidently, 'If you are willing to pay me that sort of money I guarantee to market this product successfully.'

He was not amused. 'You want to earn more than I earn,' he commented, and I replied:

'I don't know what *you* do here, but *I* guarantee to make the new catalogue a success. You can get a Volkswagen for less than a Mercedes, but with a Mercedes you get better quality.'

Without my realising it, a door had opened behind me and a man had walked in – a smallish guy with a strange-looking head. He was Manfred Sadlowski, the publisher of the magazine, and he had overheard the last few minutes of the interview. Helex had basically already ruled me out because of my financial demands – and I had probably been coming on too strong for him. I guessed he thought that if I became established I might threaten his own position.

Sadlowski said, 'Herr Moll, I would like to talk to you in my office.'

I went up with him and sat down. He said, 'I overheard you and I liked what you said.' He then showed me the layout of the new catalogue and asked: 'Do you think you can sell it?'

'Yes.'

'What makes you think so?'

'Simple. You can sell anything if you are the right entrepreneur and if you have the talent for selling. It's not a matter of what you sell, it's a matter of how you sell it. I am a salesman and, without being big-headed, I am one of the best. I can sell this for you.'

'Herr Moll, I think you have just talked yourself into a job.'

Two days later I received confirmation. I was employed. The conditions were 3000 marks a month ($1700) plus commission. Up to the first Dm100,000 I was to get 6 per cent commission. After that, to Dm180,000, it was 8 per cent. Over Dm200,000 it was 12 per cent. In the long run I would earn more than Dm5000 a month – good money. I worked with Mönch for two years selling this and other publications, meeting clients in the arms business and attending various defence exhibitions. All the time my long-term aim was to become an independent arms dealer and this was the perfect way into the business, getting to know the products and the companies and meeting people. I travelled all over Germany, Austria and Switzerland.

But while my work was flourishing, my marriage was going badly. At my age I did not have it in me to devote myself to a single partner, and all the travelling gave me plenty of chances to fool around. Things came to a head when we went to Trinidad to visit Doreen's family, something we did every year. She has a beautiful sister. The third time we went it was carnival and the place went crazy. Her sister made fairly obvious advances to me at the carnival ball at the Hilton and we started an affair. At the airport at the end of the holiday the sister burst into tears in front of the whole family. It was extremely embarrassing.

Doreen and I went back to Germany and I said I thought it was better if we got divorced. But Doreen cried for hours and in the end I felt sorry for her, because I have this soft spot where women are concerned. We decided to wait and see what happened. That year we went on holiday to Scotland and London – a place we'd visited many times, because Doreen had worked there before she moved to Germany.

In London I used to go out at night with various excuses and meet girls. Once or twice I'd have sex with them in the back of the car. But I don't want people to get the wrong idea about my attitude to women. I don't regard them as sex objects: far from it. I love women and I enjoy being with them for all sorts of reasons. I like to give them pleasure in many ways, not just physical. But by now it was clear that Doreen and I were not hitting it off. She was a few years older than me and maybe that was part of the reason. In any case, it upset me to see things breaking up and I was releasing my frustration in other ways.

By the time we went back to Germany my mind was made up on two things: I had to get divorced and I had to move to London. Apart from being dazzled by the city, I had learned by now that it was where most of the world's arms business is transacted. Dealing in arms is not against the law in Britain, as it is in some other places. In Germany you need a licence even to do the paper work. In Britain you can do what you like so long as you act only as a broker and do not actually keep any stocks – if you do that, you need special premises and security. And another point in London's favour is that Arabs, who are the best customers for the illicit arms market, feel more comfortable there than in most other western cities.

Equipment is of course available to armies through conventional government-to-government purchases. There are two main reasons why many prefer to go through freelance dealers. One is that supplying arms is a public act of support for a regime – and in some circumstances that can be politically embarrassing. That was what dictated the United States government's *modus operandi* in providing arms to Iran. The second reason is that it is harder to siphon commissions from official, above-board government trans-actions; and with such large sums of money changing hands, many people think they have a right to a generous cut.

A lot of inexperienced dealers come unstuck over the matter of commissions. When you're discussing a deal with a government official in the Middle East you must never directly broach the subject of his rake-off. If you do you could end up in the cooler, and even if that doesn't happen the deal will certainly be called off. The time to approach it is when all the other details have been fixed. Then you say you would like to appoint a local agent to handle the arrangements from that end, and does your client by any chance know a suitable firm or person? Your man will give you the name of a company that is almost certainly run by a relative or a colleague. So everything is kept in the family – while at the same time it is all above board.

*

Doreen was difficult about a divorce but I sold her the idea of moving to England. I said I would go over there first and look for a job. I contacted Jane's, the British military publishers who produce a series of plump books about the world's weapons. They were interested and asked me to go to London for an interview. They were launching a new magazine called *Jane's Defence Weekly* and wanted me to market it for them in Germany and Austria, although I would be based in London.

I was staying at the Royal Garden Hotel in Kensington and in the evenings I would go to discotheques to meet girls. Four nights before I was due to leave, I went to a pub near the hotel. As I stood at the bar drinking my Guinness I saw two young Thai women sitting at a table, talking rapidly in their own language. One was attractive and one was plain – I find that's often the way when two women go out together. And invariably the way to the pretty one is through the plain one.

The pretty one went to the ladies' room and I sat at their table and began talking to the other one. When the pretty one came back I was introduced. Her name was Noi. I managed to persuade her to get rid of her friend. We dropped the friend home and I took Noi to Thursday's, a disco, where we stayed until closing time at 3.30 a.m.

I offered Noi a lift to her home near Maida Vale. Several times I asked her to come back to my room at the Royal Gardens, but it didn't work and I could tell it was no use trying any more. A good salesman knows when he has to pull back a bit. The whole act of meeting a woman is basically the same thing as selling something, but here you're selling yourself. Not everybody looks like Paul Newman, certainly not me. Those of us unfortunate enough not to look like Paul Newman have basically to talk our way into a woman's heart – or bed, or whatever. This usually works as far as I'm concerned, because selling is my business.

But not this time. I sat in my car with her – the Opel Commodore 2.5 litre that I'd driven over from Germany – and we talked till 6 a.m. I was trying to convince her that I was the best thing that had ever happened to her. The trouble was that she was engaged; funnily enough to another German man she'd met in London, when she'd been working at the Inter-Continental Hotel. She said, 'Why can't we be just friends?' I said there was no way I could be just friends with such a beautiful woman. I gave her the phone number of the hotel and my room number and said, 'If you think there can be more between us than friends, call me at lunch time and we'll see what happens.'

I went back to the hotel totally shattered, and went to sleep. Noi's phone call woke me and we arranged to meet after I'd had a shower. I took her walking through Covent Garden. I asked her to sit down at a café and went round the corner and bought her a bunch of red roses. It always works. It's said that flowers are the key to a woman's heart and it's right. She opened up much more, until after a while I realised I was getting emotionally involved. We spent the next four days together until I had to go back to Germany. I took her phone number and gave her my office number because I was still living with Doreen. Back in Germany, I resigned my job from the end of the year and convinced Doreen I would have to go to London by myself for a year: she could follow me later. I was trying to separate without hurting her too much.

I used to call Noi regularly and she would call me. I was to leave Germany to come to England in the New Year, but ten days before Christmas I got a phone call from Noi saying, 'Guess what. I'm coming over.' I had to pretend I was pleased but in truth it created a difficult problem. I was still living with my wife and Noi didn't know I was married. If I told her not to come she would get suspicious.

I had an idea. There was a man working for the company who had a flat in Bonn but also lived with his parents further away in Aachen. I asked him, 'Are you going home for Christmas?' He said he was.

'When?'

'In two days' time.'

'What about leaving tomorrow? Here are 300 marks. Give me the key to your place.' He guessed why I needed it and smiled as he handed it over.

I told Doreen I had to go out of town for a week on business. I went home and packed, left my suitcase in the Bonn apartment building, then went to pick up Noi from the airport. I told people in the office to say I was away when my wife called. Amazingly, it worked. I even managed to spend part of Christmas Eve with Noi and another part with Doreen and my parents – although only at the expense of eating four large festive meals and making numerous breakneck trips on the motorway between Bonn and Cologne. It was like a Jacques Tati film. It came as a great relief when Noi and I left on Christmas night for London, where we stayed at a modest hotel near the Royal Garden.

This was December and I was not due to start work for Jane's until June. I used the intervening six months to make contacts in the arms trade and set up possible deals. The problem with this business is that any deal takes time. Nothing happens in a month. So, using the skill I had learned in the army, I drove trucks to make money and conserve my resources.

I signed up with a drivers' bureau, where you call in and they give you an assignment for the next day. There was one job I remember clearly. I'd been told to report at 6 a.m. to a yard near the Elephant and Castle in south London. I was driving round one of the big roundabouts on my way there when a guy in a Jaguar cut in front of me and forced me to brake. I shook my fist at him and stuck close to his tail making faces. He was furious. I was enjoying myself until I noticed with surprise that he turned into the same goods yard as I was heading for. And I was even more alarmed to find, after I had introduced myself, that he was the boss, the man in charge of giving out the jobs. He did not see the funny side at all.

'I hope you drive my truck better than you drive your car,' he barked. 'Yours is the one at the very end of that line.'

There was a row of perhaps two dozen nearly new Volvo units with well-equipped cabins. But at the very end of the line was a single battered old Leyland. He had given me the worst unit in the yard.

The job was to drive to a depot near the North Circular Road, load up with thirty tons of frozen orange juice and deliver it somewhere north of London. The unit did not like the weight of the load at all. It was straining up every small hill, a real horror to drive. My route took me through a village on a very steep hill, with a zebra crossing half-way up it. I knew that if I had to stop I would have the devil's own job getting started again. Sure enough an elderly woman stepped on the crossing as I approached it. I stopped. And when the time came to move on – nothing. The engine revved noisily but the wheels stayed firmly where they were. I was stuck and there was nothing I could do about it.

It was quite a busy street and a queue of traffic had already built up behind me. I looked back and saw that it would soon stretch out of sight. Drivers were honking their horns. A young policeman poked his head into the cab.

'Any problem, sir?' he asked. 'You seem to be causing a traffic jam.'

It never pays to be rude to policemen. My rule is not to brush with authority unless I have to. So I did not give the obvious smart response but explained politely what the trouble was.

'You'll have to back down the hill, then, won't you sir?'

It was a long job. First the policeman had to move the dozens of cars behind me. Finally I was able to reverse down the hill and park the truck off the road. I phoned the man at the depot:

'Your clapped-out truck is here,' I told him angrily. 'You can come and collect it.' And I took a taxi home.

I drove trucks for two months, always wondering whether any of my business contacts would spot me and recognise me. That would not have been good for my image at all. Then in June 1981 I started working at Jane's. It's a very old, well-established British company based in City Road, just north of the financial centre of the City itself. It is a traditional type of firm that does business the old-fashioned way. I came with very different ideas, as a modern entrepreneur who believes in innovation and the hard sell. I thought the place needed shaking up and this caused some of the older people to resent me. Jane's believed that it was the Rolls-Royce of the defence market and that as such it didn't have to advertise or do any marketing. I told them that even Rolls-Royce have to advertise and make people aware of what they have to offer.

When I joined Jane's their revenue from Germany was less than $45,000 a year. I told them that to boost that I needed to go on sales trips and to exhibitions and above all I needed an expense account. That went against their custom and raised a few eyebrows but reluctantly they agreed. It wasn't a big enough sum but I told myself that if I was successful it would get bigger.

I was in fact extremely successful with *Jane's Defence Weekly* and managed to get a very large budget. I increased advertising sales in Germany to over $750,000 in a few months. I also helped my private business by going to Germany several times and to international defence exhibitions, where I used to entertain potential clients for my own deals, as well as for Jane's. Taking people out for a good and expensive dinner is a vital part of a salesman's technique, especially when you're dealing with middle-level employees. You need to make them feel important: that's what they like. It's a normal thing in selling, but it wasn't easy to convince my bosses at Jane's that it was worth the money they were spending on it.

After I had been working there for about six months came a big moment – my first successful independent deal. Military supplies are not always arms. There is also money to be made from quartermasters' equipment. That first deal was to supply 50,000 pairs of army boots for Saudi Arabia. A German friend of mine put me in touch with the Saudis. He asked me if I could find boots for them and I said yes, of course. I was a good enough salesman to know that your first reaction to any request must always be yes, even if you haven't the least idea how to go about it.

I phoned Ian Hogg, the editor of *Jane's Infantry Weapons*. He put me on to a company in Norwich, J. R. Woodford, that dealt in cheap but good-quality quartermasters' supplies, many of the items coming from Taiwan. I phoned and introduced myself to Jeff Woodford and asked for a quote. It took him a week or so, then he quoted $14 a pair. I added $2 for myself and passed it on to my German friend, who passed it on to the Saudis. Nothing happened for a long time, which is usual in this business: you give a quote and they sit on it for months. I never count my money before it is in the bank. I was quite excited because this was my first deal and I was hopeful, but even so I did not let my expectations climb too high.

Finally a request came for samples. They looked good to me. I sent them to Germany by courier and there was a frustrating delay because the couriers lost them. Irritating though this was, I was building up valuable experience of coping with the much greater frustrations of dealing in military hardware. After four weeks I heard that the Saudis were comparing my samples with others, and two weeks later I learned that we had the order.

My pleasure was quickly dampened when I heard about the rival bidders. An American firm had offered inferior boots at $24 a pair, while the Koreans were cheaper but, as is usual, of very low quality. It meant that I could have still won the contract if I had charged an extra four or five dollars a pair – making an extra $200,000 on the deal. But it's all a part of the game, and is one of the reasons why everyone in it is so secretive. No dealer will ever tell the customer the source of his supply, in case they start dealing direct and squeeze out the middle man. So my German clients didn't want me to have any direct contact with the Saudis and I didn't want the German company to know where I was getting the boots from. You're talking about money. One thing I learned in business a long time ago is not to trust other people when there's money involved.

That is why the method of payment for all these deals – for quartermasters' supplies as well as arms – is so elaborate. Every deal starts with a request from the purchaser to the dealer, who responds with a quotation. The buyer then has to satisfy himself about both the product offered and the dealer offering it. He needs to be sure that the dealer can in fact get his hands on the goods required. Having assured himself of that, the buyer will issue a pre-advised letter of credit, which is a telex from the buyer's bank to the seller's bank saying they are willing and able to open a letter of credit for a certain sum on receipt of a performance bond, normally for about 5 per cent of the value of the contract, which is forfeited if the goods are not supplied. The seller's bank then sends a telex to the buyer's bank saying, 'We are holding the performance bond and are ready to exchange.' Then the buyer's bank sends the letter of credit to the seller's bank and the seller's bank sends the performance bond to the buyer's bank, and the deal is secured.

The letters of credit (LCs) are payable only on presentation of bills of lading proving that the goods have been loaded on to ships bound for the customer's chosen port. But even this safeguard is not watertight, as some purchasers occasionally discovered to their cost, when the ships arrived without the correct goods on board. The problem is that very few banks will accept a letter of credit that describes the product as '50,000 rounds of 155mm ammunition' or whatever. The banks know what the business is but they don't want to get involved officially. They want to cover their backsides. So, to hide the true nature of the cargo, the contract may say '20,000 tons of bricks' – very expensive bricks – or machine tools or even, in one case I heard about, Brylcreem.

And some countries – Iran especially – have been caught in an elaborate swindle based on these 'doctored' contracts or letters of credit. The customer will inspect the arms at the port where they are loaded, and find them in order. The seller has performed, so his performance bond is validated and the letter of credit is paid. But by the time the ship arrives at its destination the cargo may have changed mysteriously into the innocent items mentioned in the contract – the bricks or the Brylcreem. They were switched on the high seas, and the customer has no legal recourse, because technically the contract has been fulfilled. The result is that Iran may have enough Brylcreem to last for hundreds of years.

There was no need for such subterfuge in the case of my boots for Saudi Arabia. The Saudis opened an LC to the German company, who in turn opened a transferable LC to my bank, and then I transferred it to my supplier. But delivery of the boots took three months – so I had to wait that long for my $45,000 cut. When it finally came through I took Noi to Les A for a champagne dinner.

While this deal was slowly coming to the boil I had a chance meeting with the man who was to become my partner. It happened at the end of an eventful sales trip to Vienna that had gone a long way to confirming my view that the arms business is a passport to the good life.

Usually I invite people to lunch but this time, in the Austrian capital, I had been invited by a businessman who brought his secretary with him. She was gorgeous but I had to spend most of the lunch talking to him about advertising in Jane's and about some communications equipment that he might be able to supply for a potential customer of mine. I was staying at the Hilton and after lunch I invited the pair of them back for a drink. The man had to leave but I took his secretary. Just before she, too, had to go I asked her what she was doing that night. Nothing special, she replied. I invited her for dinner at eight.

At six I went to the bar by the lobby where there was a special area set aside for a party for Hilton Club guests. I'm a member of the club – it's a perk for regular clients – and while I was talking to some of the hotel managers I knocked back half a dozen large gin-and-tonics almost without noticing it. They were free, after all. Suddenly someone tapped me on the shoulder.

'Have you forgotten about me?' my dinner guest asked. In fact I had, but I denied it passionately. In any case, I was unlikely to forget her quickly again because she was wearing the slinkiest and sexiest black leather outfit I'd ever seen.

She suggested a Russian restaurant called the Firebird, a

picturesque place with wooden tables and music. As soon as we sat down they brought us a carafe of iced vodka each. We had an assortment of starters, then bortsch. By that time I was completely drunk and asked the waiter, 'Bring us a pound of beluga caviar, hot blinis, sour cream and Russian champagne.'

Somewhere in the middle of that dinner my memory of the evening blanks out. The next thing I remember is waking up with a terrible hangover and something moving in the bed alongside me. She was leaning on one arm, looking at me challengingly. I had already noticed that she was well built – it's the kind of thing that doesn't escape me – but not until now had I realised how superb her bosom was. I moved closer to touch it lightly and she smiled. She was obviously determined that the night should not be wasted, in spite of my over-indulgence. For a couple of hours I forgot my hangover and made the best of it. She was the most uninhibited woman I have ever slept with, and made it a morning worth remembering. Then I found in my pocket the staggering bill for the Russian restaurant, which made doubly sure I would not forget it quickly.

There was a postscript to my little adventure. Two days later I went back to Jane's and found everyone grinning at me. There had been a telex from Vienna that said: 'Darling, I left my contact lenses in your room. Can you get them back for me?' At Jane's I was already getting a reputation as a playboy, and that confirmed it. My divorce from Doreen had come through but I was not entirely free, as I was sharing a house with Noi.

It was while coming back from Vienna by British Airways that I met John Saunders. I try to get aisle seats on aeroplanes because of my height and even in Club Class there is not really enough room for my legs. Across the aisle was a small man, about five foot five, very thin, with wispy hair, wearing glasses and smoking heavily. Next to him was a man who was unmistakably Middle Eastern. The small man was wearing a very expensive Piaget watch, and his neighbour a diamond Rolex, as well as gold jewellery. As a salesman in a high-priced field, these are the little things you learn to notice: you look at their shoes and watch, to see if they really mean business.

The impression of money was definitely there. I thought I might be on to something interesting; so I introduced myself.

The small man said his name was John Saunders and he had lived in the Middle East for eighteen years. The man next to him was from Lebanon – a relative, I later discovered, of Saunders' Lebanese wife. In the Middle East most business is done through family connections.

'What business are you in?' he asked.

'The defence business,' I replied.

'Sounds interesting,' he said. 'We're coming to England to look for some equipment for the Christians in Lebanon. Do you have any contacts for equipment?' I said I had.

Saunders said he had until six months ago been working in the United Arab Emirates (UAE) procuring supplies for its armed forces. Now he was in business on his own and was trying to get some supplies for the Christians in Lebanon. He gave me no real details, only the kind of bullshit that's common in this business about the kinds of deals you're doing and the sums of money you're making. We arranged that he would call me next day and we would see if there was anything we could do together. When he called he invited me for dinner at his club, Les Ambassadeurs. I had heard about Les A and passed it many times, but had never been asked inside before. All I knew was its reputation for being expensive – too expensive for me, I had always assumed. I was greatly impressed, not to say dazzled, to be invited there.

Before dinner we sat in the oak-panelled library near the fireplace. Saunders handed me a paper which was basically a shopping list. He wanted:

200,000 60mm mortar rounds
100,000 81mm mortar rounds
2000 60mm mortars

1000 81mm mortars
150,000 155mm shells

plus some quartermasters' supplies and other smaller items. The total value was about $24½ million. I looked at the list and said yes. I didn't tell him I hadn't actually completed any deals for hardware yet. If I'd said 'No,' or 'I'll see,' he would not have been impressed. I was in a position of having to create a can-do image, then live up to it.

We had a very nice dinner – Chateaubriand for two and the wine that he always ordered, a fine vintage claret. We'd had about seven gin-and-tonics beforehand and then a couple of Armagnacs afterwards. We talked about the deal and its mechanics. I would supply the quotation and he would pass it on to the people in Lebanon and they would place an order. It sounded good – but I know never to count money before it's in the bank account.

Under the influence of the drink, John told me some of the secrets of his craft in the UAE army. When a contract was to be let, five or six companies would tender for it. In return for a large commission he would tell one of the companies what was in the sealed bids of the others – the prices, conditions, etc. – so they could better them. He would share the commission with his superior officer. That is the way business is done in the Middle East.

John was wealthy, worth about £1 million. He had a house in Shirley, near Croydon, where he lived with his wife and two sons. While in the Middle East he developed diabetes. He said he had a lot of contacts in the UAE and the Gulf states, including a man in Abu Dhabi named Hamid al-Shamzi, who used to be a colonel in the army and was still an active member of the secret police.

The dinner went on till nearly midnight. I agreed to supply the quotations and spent the next two or three days phoning contacts. First I got a price on the mortars and mortar rounds from Austrian companies I had known for some years through my work with Mönch and Jane's. Through other contacts, I worked through the list.

Getting a quotation for arms is not as easy as it sounds.

First you have to convince the supplier that you're a genuine customer and you can only do that if they know you. Once I'd created the impression there was a serious requirement, they gave me a quotation. I called John and said: 'I have everything. Where shall we meet?' It was Les A again, this time for lunch. I gave him the quote and he seemed very pleased. The price was realistic and the goods were available, but the delivery time was a bit long – three to six months, which is normal if you buy from a manufacturer and not from stock. But customers are always in a hurry.

John said he was going to Lebanon shortly and would hand the quotations to the Christian army. Then, for the first time, we discussed a possible more permanent business relationship. It was my idea. I sought to convince Saunders that we should become partners. I had thought it through carefully. Here was a man who had two important things – money and contacts in the Middle East, where there are a lot of customers for the things I sell. He was hungry for new business. I would also soon have some money from the boots deal – although not nearly as much as John – and I had contacts with arms suppliers. We could be of immense value to each other. As for myself, why couldn't I leave the staff of Jane's but do the same job for them as a freelance, while at the same time running my own company? It was worth thinking about.

John was in Lebanon for three or four weeks. While he was away I went on a four-day trip to Genoa where I met Vittorio, who worked as a freelance agent for Jane's in Italy. He held agencies for some thirty publications and had a fine office in the middle of Genoa, with a staff of six. I was very impressed with his operation: there was obviously money coming in. I told him I was thinking of setting up my own firm, like his, and he said he would help me to get business from French and Spanish military publications. In this business it's essential to know people. Everything is done by recommendation.

I saw two possibilities. One was to devote myself exclusively to selling arms: but because deals are slow coming to the boil, and because I didn't have enough funds available to tide me over, I wanted some regular income. You never know how long it takes for a big deal to come through. So I set up two parallel businesses, as an advertising salesman and a dealer in military equipment, arms and quartermasters' supplies.

As a freelance agent, your revenue is basically 30 per cent of the advertising you sell, but you normally have to pass half of that on to the agency that books the space and does the art work and layout for the client. That leaves you with 15 per cent – not bad because I was estimating a revenue at Jane's at that time of about £400,000 a year. The other four accounts would be smaller but would amount to £200,000 on top of that, plus further growth potential and a possible expansion into commercial advertising. So here was a business that could create an annual income of at least £100,000, which is not at all bad – but that is just what I call the bread and butter. The jam was the arms deals.

I calculated that I need only spend about two days a week on the advertising business. Once a year I would see the executives of the companies in London or Germany and for the rest of the year all I had to do was schedule the advertising of the bigger companies and drum up business with the smaller ones. For the remainder of the week I could work on the arms transactions. The advertising work also gave me cover. The arms business is a bit dodgy but I could travel to defence exhibitions and meetings on the advertising pretext, and nobody would suspect anything. But I could not go it alone because it was too much work and I did not have enough capital to hire two or three employees.

John came back from Lebanon without an order, but he said it looked hopeful: the prospects were still good. In the end that deal fell through, but it took a long time before we knew we were not going to make any headway. In the Middle East it takes an age to come to any decision and when a place is in total chaos, like Lebanon, it takes even longer. On a trip in the Middle East a while later I met an American at my hotel bar. He was swigging his beer in great gulps, as beads of sweat appeared on his forehead. He was swearing quietly to himself, a picture of total frustration.

'Jee-zus Christ,' he kept muttering. 'Jee-zus.'

'What's up?' I asked him, as he obviously wanted me to do.

'It makes you want to cry,' he confided. 'The only thing you hear around here is IBM.'

'IBM?' I queried. 'You mean the American computer company? Are they competitors of yours?'

He smiled without much humour and took another mouthful of beer.

'No,' he said. 'I don't mean them. IBM – you know, Inshallah Bukaresh Malek. It's Arabic and it means "By Allah's will, tomorrow . . . maybe." It's all you ever hear around here.'

I bought him another drink. I had not been doing business with the Arabs for long at that time, but I was already beginning to discover what he meant.

As soon as John was back I sat him down and raised again the prospect of our going into partnership. By now I had researched the possibilities and suggested that we should establish two companies together, one a British company for more orthodox trading and the other one a Panamanian offshore company for the arms deals. I would bring into the business all the advertising agencies, with an annual income of between £80,000 and £120,000. John would bring in some cash – we were then talking about £30,000 – and his contacts in the Middle East. After a couple of days we came to an agreement.

My next task was to convince Jane's to give me their agencies even though I would leave their staff. I had only been with them for ten months. They weren't too keen but I showed them that they would actually gain. My large expense account helped: they were relieved to be no longer responsible for it. After a week of negotiation I succeeded in convincing the managing director that it was the best thing that could happen to him and to Jane's, and we signed a deal.

John and I launched International Services Bellfine Ltd, a

ready-made company that I bought off the shelf at Companies House. This was to be the onshore British company that dealt with the advertising market. For arms trading, I established International Procurement and Sales in Panama. We decided that we did not need the prestige of West End offices because they are expensive and parking is a nightmare. You seldom see clients in the office anyway: you meet them in bars and restaurants. All you need is somewhere with a secretary, a telex and a telephone. We established the office in a flat where I had lived for a while in Teignmouth Road in Cricklewood, a run-down district of north-west London. It was part of the ground floor of a large Edwardian house and not in any sense a prestige address – but it sounded better when I put 'Suite 4' on the letterheads, instead of 'Flat 4'. It was convenient for where Noi and I were now living, in Abercorn Road on the borders of Hampstead and Mill Hill. John and I went out and spent £3000 on desks, stationery, visiting cards and equipment, and we were in business.

John's friend Hamid al-Shamzi was appointed our agent in Abu Dhabi, with a brief to check on the requirements of the armed services. But it was all small stuff. He had a contract to supply the UAE army with 100,000 survival packs, soon due for renewal. I thought we would make up our own ration packs – a seven-day pack with a shelf life of four years. I went out acquiring various products for it, but I was in effect just shopping for groceries. I could not pretend that it was the glamorous, dangerous life I had dreamed of when I entered the business. I was longing to sew up my first deal in actual weapons.

That came as a result of contacts I made during my first trip with John Saunders, to the Hanover air show in 1984. We were staying at the Maritime Hotel, one of the central venues in the city, the sort of place where you meet people who lead you on to other people. John was supposed to do deals – that's why I took him as a partner. He was still working then on the Lebanon transaction but they eventually got their weapons from the eastern bloc. The problem, as I discovered too late, was that although John knew people in the Middle East he wasn't able to transfer knowing them into actual business. He wasn't a salesman at all. When I went to America in 1986 I was in the process of separating, of getting him out of the business, because he was a waste of money and didn't really produce anything, although he took half the profits.

After the Hanover show I was contacted by a German friend looking for fifty machine guns for the Chilean army. I got them from stock in a warehouse in Sri Lanka, belonging to a British arms dealer. Because they were in stock they were rather cheap and I was able to make some money on the deal – about £30,000. This was not bad for a fairly small transaction but even if it had been a lot less I would still have been exultant, because it was my first deal in hardware. The guns were shipped from Sri Lanka to Chile. They never came near to England – and nor did my payment.

This was completed about eight months after the Saudi boots deal and in the meantime I had been working on other hardware possibilities. Word was being spread about me and I was now getting around eight enquiries a week, mostly by guarded telephone calls. One was from the Iranian Razabi. He said the Iranians wanted NBC suits (to protect soldiers against nuclear, bacteriological and chemical warfare) because the Iraqis had begun using chemical weapons. Iran also wanted 155mm shells, mortars and mortar rounds.

I phoned friends who confirmed that, as far as they knew, Razabi was legitimate, and then I looked around for sources of supply. For the 155mm shells I got a quotation from the Greek Cartridge and Powder Company. For the NBC suits I got some quotes from an English company and one in Taiwan. But the British NBC suits are on the list of controlled goods. They're used by the British army, so technically they're classified and you need an export licence for them. Eventually I got them from Taiwan.

The 155mm HE rounds usually retail for between $260 and $280 for each shell. Razabi wanted between 150,000 and 200,000 of them. From Greece, the problem was delivery times. One of the drawbacks of dealing with the Iranian armed forces is that they have no long-term planning as such. They don't work out their need on the basis of how many shells they use per day, but wait until someone says, 'We're getting low on shells. Let's get some.' That means they always need to buy from stock rather than place an order with a manufacturer. In a war like this I guessed that they use about 10,000 shells a day in a large-scale attack. Eventually I supplied them with some 20,000 shells which were in stock and available in Portugal.

They wanted mortars and mortar rounds, which I couldn't help them with because there were no stocks available. In the end they bought them from Korea, although I warned Razabi that Korean equipment is of poor quality. Sure enough, when they started using them they found the charge was too low and the mortars fell on their own front line instead of on the Iraqis. I would never quote Korean equipment to any customer. I believe that I supply quality and I don't want to have people after my backside. Quality is expensive, though. Korean 60mm mortar shells can be had for $25, where, for example, those made in Austria would be $50 or $60.

I had realised by then that there was a lot of money in Iran and this war. I had no conscience about it. Iraq started the war and Iran is defending itself. Under the Shah, thousands of people disappeared or were tortured – so the Ayatollah's revolution was justified, and naturally the country is taking time to settle down. But basically it's a business and I don't make judgements between customers. I would have supplied the former Chilean regime, under the Communist Dr Allende, as well as this right-wing dictatorship of Pinochet. But I would draw the line at supplying the Contra rebels in Nicaragua because they are trying to overthrow a legitimate government.

I don't sell arms to terrorists. I don't think the world can be safe for any of us if they're allowed to operate freely. Anybody who encourages them is being irresponsible. That's the difference between me and the US Government. It says it doesn't support terrorists but in practice it does. I say I don't sell arms to terrorists and I stick to it.

Mind you, I would have considered myself pro-American if you had asked me before my experiences in New York. To be truthful, politics never interested me much, although I suppose that by most standards you would say I was on the right, because I believe in everyone standing up for himself and making his way by his own efforts. That's certainly how I organise my own life. But I believe that whatever political party is in power they are devoted mainly to their own careers and success. Their interest is to be re-elected if they're democratic politicians, and just to stay in power if they are not. But there's one practical advantage in dealing with governments and not with guerrilla groups: governments are more likely to be able to afford to pay you.

To make the most of John's contacts in the Middle East, I visited Abu Dhabi, Dubai and Oman in 1984. I was with a Pakistani friend called Asif Mahmoud, a nephew of the late President Bhutto. He was tall and overweight but a first-rate womaniser. He was essentially a fixer. While Bhutto was in power he made a nice commission from an American company for selling Hercules aircraft to Pakistan. He had an expensive flat near Harrods. I took him with me because he used to know an influential man called Yahya Nasib, who became my agent in Oman afterwards. He used to pick up women for Yahya, so he had quite a lot of influence over him.

I bought two first-class tickets London/Abu Dhabi/Muscat/London/Paris/London: the Paris detour was to visit the big summer air show there. The British Airways flight to Abu Dhabi left at 8 p.m. John took me to Heathrow in his black Rolls-Royce and we picked up Asif at his flat on the way. We were working on a deal with Abu Dhabi for ration packs. In Dubai I was selling mine detectors and I took a sample with me. The Oman part of the trip was basically for reconnaissance.

It turned out that we had timed the trip badly: it was during Ramadan so it was hard to get a drink. We had been warned about it and I made the most of the free gin on the plane, before I went to sleep. It was dark when we arrived at Abu Dhabi airport, a fantastic multi-coloured citadel. My visa was waiting and after I picked it up I walked through to collect my luggage, including the mine detector, two bottles of Dom Perignon, a bottle of gin and a bottle of Johnny Walker Black Label whisky. Although Abu Dhabi is not completely dry like Saudi Arabia, they don't like to see that in customs during Ramadan.

Hamid al-Shamzi, John's friend and our local agent, was there to meet me. A chubby man of medium height, he dresses elegantly when in London but in his home country he wears something that looks like a sheet, hanging loosely around him. He's a real Arab: always friendly on the surface, but you never know what he is really thinking.

When he saw what I was carrying he said, 'Oh dear, what do you have there?'

'A mine detector.'

'And what's in that bag?'

'Booze.'

'Oh dear.'

We went to see the head customs officer in a small office. He clucked when I told him I had a mine detector. Hamid said I would have to get clearance for it and I had to leave it there.

It was early morning when I arrived at the Inter-Continental Hotel, a high-rise building in its own small park nine miles from Abu Dhabi airport and just away from the town centre. But it was June and even at that time of the day it was very hot, about 33° Centigrade. I had no appointments at all on that first day so I went up to my pleasantly air-conditioned suite and slept for a couple of hours, then got up and took a beer from the mini-bar in the room. I felt hungry, put on some bathing trunks and shorts and went downstairs. During Ramadan Arabs get up for a meal before dawn and then don't have anything to eat, drink or smoke until dusk. So only two of the hotel's four restaurants were open.

I went to the poolside restaurant and had shish kebab and rice and a huge glass of mango juice. It was now even hotter and I decided to get a suntan at the beach club, a short walk from the hotel, past the marina with its fabulously expensive yachts, which look as if they had never been used and possibly had not. The beach bar was closed because of Ramadan so I went straight into the sea, which was around the same temperature as the air. It was like swimming in warm soup, not a bit refreshing. After about half an hour in the water I was just getting hotter and hotter so I walked back to the hotel pool, which was chilled. About two dozen air stewardesses were lounging round the pool but it was too hot to take an interest.

After about four hours outside I went back to the poolside restaurant, had another glass of mango juice, and suddenly felt my skin was getting too small for my body. My complexion is fair and tender and I had caught a beautiful sunburn. I went to my suite and spent half an hour sitting in front of the air conditioner, then dozed away the afternoon in bed. At 6 p.m. I got up and had a shower, felt a bit better, got dressed and went down to the main restaurant to eat. After dinner I took the lift to the top floor. During Ramadan each big hotel in the area has a drinking room for non-Moslems. I rang the bell. A Pakistani waiter eyed me suspiciously, then, recognising that I was not a Moslem, opened the door, although with a show of sullen reluctance. Inside, the room was heavy with smoke. It was packed. Every foreigner in the hotel was there, most of them from the international oil companies. The only alternative was to drink alone from the mini-bar in your room and I prefer boozing in company; but it was unbearably boring, with nothing to do but watch videos on the TV. At midnight I decided to call it a day.

The sunburn had eased but the drink made me a bit sluggish at 7.30 next morning, when Hamid picked me up and drove me to his office to discuss a number of small deals, including the one for ration packs. The working day effectively ends there at 11 a.m. After we'd done our business we talked about women for a while – I never did more than talk about them for the whole trip – then he drove me back to the hotel for lunch while he went home to sleep. During Ramadan, Arabs tend to look very tired by noon.

After lunch I was to meet some relatives of John's wife. We went to the Meridian Hotel beach club, a bit more relaxed than the Inter-Continental, where they don't let you take drinks from the restaurants to the pool. The Meridian pool was crowded, mainly with Lebanese. I met a beautiful dark-eyed girl sitting by the edge of the sea, letting the water lap round her ankles. We talked for about an hour and got on tremendously. I felt I had a chance with her and, though I could feel my skin shrinking again, convinced myself it was worth it. The time came for me to make the crucial move. I invited her for dinner at my hotel. She smiled sadly. 'My husband wouldn't approve,' she said. Conceding defeat, I decided to leave straightaway.

I walked to the road to try to get a taxi and finally one came along. It was a battered, filthy car driven by an old unshaven man who looked like a Bedouin. He was very ancient and didn't speak English. He drove at fifteen miles an hour with one arm outside the window and the other on the steering wheel, spitting out of the window every twenty seconds. He was driving in the middle of the road, blocking two lanes, and swearing at other drivers. A trip that normally takes fifteen minutes took half an hour, and there was no air-conditioning. When I finally arrived back at the hotel I dashed upstairs to my mercifully cool suite. At the hotel shop later on, I bought emergency supplies of suntan lotion.

Next day I had arranged a meeting with Sheik Faisal bin Sultan al-Kasimi, from Sharjah. I was discussing deals for arms, uniforms, ration packs and other supplies, and later a single order came out of it. On the Sheik's recommendation I went back to the customs office near the airport to get my mine detector. This time the head of customs smiled and said there was no problem. 'We need some metal detectors here at customs,' he told me. 'Can you quote for them?'

All this time Asif had been making his own arrangements and was staying at a different hotel, the Holiday Inn. That evening, before we left for Dubai, I went with him to the Holiday Inn drinking room where I consumed perhaps ten large gin-and-tonics. Somebody told us there was one discotheque open in town – at the Central Hotel. Desperate, we took a taxi there. It was true that it was open, but it was dead, nobody inside. I made a note to pick the time of my next Middle East trip more carefully. Ramadan is bad news out there.

By the time we got the taxi back I was seriously drunk. I asked the taxi driver if there was action anywhere.

'What do you mean?' he asked, puzzled.

My reply was slurred. 'Drink, women,' I said carelessly.

The driver started shouting. He was a Pakistani but Asif said he was from the mountain region and a very strict Moslem. Asif was terrified.

'You know what he's going to do now?' he said, shaking. 'He's going to take us to the police because we are drunk. He will collect a good reward for it.'

Suddenly my head became clearer as I focused on the danger. I did not relish the prospect of an encounter with the Abu Dhabi police. Hamid would have had us freed soon enough but I could do without the hassle.

'No,' I said quietly. 'He isn't going to do any such thing.'

I was sitting behind the driver. I put my arm round his throat and said, 'Two choices, friend. Either you stop the car or I break your neck.' He took the first option and we got another taxi back to the hotel.

Next day we had a car arranged to take us on the two-hour drive to Dubai. There was no point in flying. There is a helicopter service but I wanted to see the famous desert road. It is entirely barren and desolate, except for the occasional shack by the side of the road selling refreshments – though not during Ramadan. By the roadside were fifty or sixty wrecked cars, some of them new-looking Mercedes and Rolls-Royces. I was told they had been involved in accidents, probably with the camels that lumber across the road at night, oblivious of the traffic. Hitting the beasts at 80 m.p.h. is no joke.

We had reserved two rooms at the Dubai Hilton – not as nice as the Sheraton but near the procurement offices of the army. I had arranged to meet Major Barnett, the Englishman in charge of procurement for the Dubai armed forces. I gave him the mine detector that had caused me so much trouble at the Abu Dhabi customs. The army tested it and eventually ordered ten at about $3000 each. In the afternoon Asif had a German stewardess coming to see him, a gorgeous blonde. Frustrated by my disappointment at the beach club a few days earlier, I told him to make sure I didn't get to see her in a bikini, or I would go crazy.

Next day the car was there in the morning. Asif was late, no doubt because of what he'd been doing the night before. We drove straight to Abu Dhabi airport, where we flew to Muscat by Middle East Airlines. Still no drink, because of Ramadan, but I had my own bottle of gin and ordered some tonic to go with it. The Arab passengers were horrified, partly for religious reasons but mostly, I guessed, from envy. I let them look on disapprovingly. What did it matter to me?

At Muscat I still had with me two bottles of champagne and another bottle of gin I'd bought duty-free at Abu Dhabi. The customs man had heard them clink and couldn't wait to get me. When I said I had nothing to declare, he took my bag and passport and sent me to an office. Asif looked worried but I was lucky because an American in front of me had been caught with eight *Playboy* magazines – a far graver offence. I was charged £40 in duty.

Yahya was at the airport to meet us in his Mercedes 1000. We stayed some six miles outside Muscat, where he has a beautiful fifty-acre estate surrounded by a high wall. There were palm trees and a swimming pool, as well as three huge bird sanctuaries. I was trying to work out how much it cost him to keep a home like this. The gardens were superb. Inside the main house was a full-size snooker table and the guest house, where I was staying, was about sixty yards away. Inside the guest house was a large gymnasium with an exercise machine and a steam bath, which seems a bit superfluous in such a hot climate.

Yahya had eight servants and many cars, including a Jaguar HE, the Mercedes, two Range Rovers and an Excalibur. He also has an estate at Aston Clinton in England, with more cars. Every year in the summer he goes to the South of France and has his Excalibur flown from

Muscat to Cannes. His company, Yahya Enterprises, is the agent for Marconi and he is involved with Costain, the developers. So he does not go short.

When we got to his estate in the early afternoon we found Yahya trying to fast for Ramadan. I slept till six, then went to the pool, where servants stand in the shadows, ready to serve drinks or fresh melon. We had dinner at 7.30. Yahya has two chefs. He acquired one of them from a London restaurant whose food he liked so much that he offered the chef double his salary to go and work for him. The food was magnificent the whole time. Four or five different main courses were all on the table at once, in the Arab style. You pick here and pick there and what's left over goes to the servants. The chef made the best bread-and-butter pudding I've ever had. I think I ate half of it. From that day on, there was a bowl of bread-and-butter pudding on the table every day. Yahya would say, 'Here comes Hermann's dinner.'

Yahya's main employee was John Adcock, a retired colonel and former British military attaché in Iraq. I met him early the following morning at his office and we went to the Muscat Ministry of Defence. They wanted ration packs as well as a particular kind of smokescreen for their navy, that burns at low temperatures. They had a problem with their modern aluminium frigates. The trouble is that aluminium breaks up at a certain temperature, as the British navy found when on the receiving end of Exocet missiles during the Falklands War. For their exercises the Omanis had to lay smoke screens and they wanted a particular kind of smoke that would not threaten their ships, which is not easy to get.

I had an agreement with a German company called Nico Pyroteknik to sell their products. They manufacture this kind of screening smoke, so we agreed that I should get a quotation from them. There were inordinate delays at both ends, partly because of the German government's initial reluctance to issue an export licence. But after several months I made a sale.

I was in Muscat for three days, of which one day was taken up with meetings and on another I had dinner with one of the Sultan's uncles. Apart from that I had nothing to do, other than visits to the steam bath, the gymnasium and the pool. The whole trip had been frustrating in many ways but it taught me a lot about dealing with Arabs. It is not easy. To begin with, you must never be under the misapprehension that an Arab is your friend. You can only be friends with an Arab if you are an Arab. They are cordial and they talk gently but they are very shrewd businessmen – and the shrewdest of all are the Lebanese.

Nothing in the Middle East is done to a European schedule. I've seen people flying out there on a Monday saying they'd be back on Thursday, but it never happens. If you want to do business you have to switch yourself to their timetable. You go to a meeting scheduled for 10 a.m. with a sheik. It is possible that he is at that very moment up in the mountains enjoying a day's falconry – a favourite pastime. He won't be an hour late but two days late and you have no choice but to wait for him. Their metabolism is different from ours.

I was looking forward to a comfortable and relaxing flight back, with no drink restrictions, but it was not to be. The British Airways office in Muscat had seen to that. When Asif and I checked in half an hour before midnight, with our two first-class reservations, they said the plane, which had come from Singapore and Australia, was overbooked. I made a fuss and told them I had to get to Paris but was about to accept their offer of free accommodation in a hotel when they found us two seats – in the economy section and right at the back. They were six of the most uncomfortable hours of my life, although BA gave us free drinks to try to make up for the inconvenience. Asif told me afterwards that I eventually fell asleep snoring, one arm across a Chinese man on my left and another across a little Chinese girl on my right. They were both too petrified to move or say anything. I woke up with a hangover and gin spilled all over the place.

In London I went home briefly. Next day, still with Asif, I flew to Paris for the air show. I had booked a suite and room at the Hilton by the Eiffel Tower – a nice hotel with easy access to the airport motorway. I got to the desk and the receptionist said, 'Sorry sir, terribly sorry.' After my experience with British Airways, I knew what to expect. 'Don't tell me. These rooms were booked three months ago. I want my suite and room now.' They said they'd moved me to the Hilton at Orly – the other side of the city from the air show. I argued but we had to go. Every day we spent two hours in a taxi, battling through the Paris traffic.

I was there to set up a deal between a German company that manufactures engines and a man from Abu Dhabi, whose name I can't mention because he'd lose his head. The UAE have thirty fast patrol craft, and for years MTU, the German manufacturers, were trying to set up a deal to replace their engines. It never came off because the German director heading the project was not able or willing to make the right commission arrangements. Before I went to Oman I had talked to someone higher up in the company and arranged that a commission could be supplied. Only the technicalities remained to be sorted out.

I set up a meeting at the Hotel George V, where I normally stay in Paris. Four of us met in a suite there – the man from MTU, myself, Asif and the customer from Abu Dhabi. We put it on paper. Each engine was worth $160,000. There were thirty of them, which makes nearly $5 million. A nice little piece of action.

Everything went perfectly at the meeting and I already had the letters for the commission, but the deal was sabotaged. Somebody in the company gave details to a rival company. Having discovered that the man from Abu Dhabi was in Paris, the rival firm sent men to confront him in his hotel suite. They threatened to report him to his government if the deal went through. People in a position like his are not supposed to meet businessmen outside their offices, except as part of a delegation. He was terrified and phoned me frantically: 'Somebody told them I am here. How can they do that? I'm going to lose my head if it becomes known. I thought I told you before that nobody must know I am here.' I assured him that I was not responsible for the leak and tried to rescue the deal but I could not. In the end I did no business in Paris at all, despite those two-hour taxi rides. In my trade you expect to lose more than you win – and that, of course, makes it all the sweeter when the fruit does finally fall from the tree into your hand.

3

The Bazaar on Victoria Street

I never used to give a second glance – often not even a first glance – to the pages in newspapers devoted to foreign news. In fact until recently I was not a great newspaper reader at all. I picked up most of my information from television if I happened to have it switched on. When I did read, it was mainly magazines on two subjects: military weapons and fast cars.

But I had not been in the arms business long before I realised that I needed to read foreign news just as a banker needs to read the financial pages and a professional gambler must study the horse-racing form. Every story about a war or guerrilla conflict, each report of casualties and belligerent statements by leaders of the rival sides, is a pointer to a potential market for the goods I sell. It is important, too, that I should understand something of the diplomatic manoeuvres behind the wars, not just by the countries chiefly involved but by the super-powers. This allows me to calculate who is supplying which side with arms, and in particular which countries find it difficult to purchase weapons through conventional channels: those are my likeliest customers.

Iran has been the most important country in that last category since 16 January 1979, when the Shah, 'the King of Kings', was overthrown by supporters of Ayatollah Khomeini. On that day, twenty years of American domination (some called it exploitation) of the country came to an end. The United States government tried to forge a businesslike relationship with the new regime – chiefly to prevent the Russians from barging in – but they could not overcome such a long and powerful legacy of resentment.

Ten months later, when the Ayatollah's fanatical supporters occupied the United States embassy and kidnapped its personnel, the Americans became sworn enemies of Iran. President Carter imposed strict economic sanctions and barred the shipment of arms there, even those already bought and paid for by the Iranian government. The year-long hostage crisis was widely believed to have led to President Carter's defeat by President Reagan in the 1980 election.

The hostages were released on the day Reagan assumed office. As a result, some sanctions were eased but the arms embargo was maintained – or at least that was what people assumed at the time. A different version, though, came from Admiral John Poindexter, who replaced Robert McFarlane as the President's National Security Adviser in December 1985. Appearing before the Congressional hearings into the Iran/Contra affair in July 1987, Poindexter said:

> Our policy was not an arms embargo against Iran. We don't just all of a sudden out of the blue decide to embargo arms to Iran. The policy objective there is an end to the Iran–Iraq war. Now one of the methods that we went about to achieve that policy objective was to reduce the flow of arms to Iran. We frankly weren't very successful.

But whatever it was called, the restriction on arms sales caused immediate difficulties to Iran's military forces. They had inherited an almost exclusively American armoury from the days of the Shah, but now they could not obtain the spare parts they needed to keep the weapons and equipment in working order. Things had been so chaotic since the revolution that nobody had the foresight to order large reserves of supplies to guard against a possible embargo. Iran was now an ideal client for freelance arms traders like me. And when, in September 1980, Iraqi troops attacked Iran to begin the long and bitter war that Poindexter referred to, the potential for business was mouth-watering.

Many fortunes were made. I wanted mine to be among them.

Until September 1987, the Iranians used to buy the bulk of their arms from the western world through what is ostensibly the offices of the Iranian National Oil Company at 4 Victoria Street in London. Regular 'exposés' were printed and broadcast about the goings-on there. I guess that the number of people engaged in the arms trade greatly exceeded the number in the oil business, but when the British government expelled Iranian diplomats after a row in the summer of 1987, the Victoria Street people were allowed to stay on. Finally they were expelled in September when a ship flying the British flag was attacked by an Iranian aircraft in the Gulf.

Sir Geoffrey Howe, the Foreign Secretary, said the Gulf incident was the final straw. However, it might be appropriate to ask why, over the previous seven years, when they had been paying lip-service to the arms embargo against Iran, the British government allowed the Victoria Street circus to continue.

It is a modern office building with thin, white vertical pillars on the front giving a suitable – though presumably coincidental – hint of the Middle East. It stands almost opposite two eminently respectable British institutions – Westminster Abbey to the east and the Department of Trade and Industry to the west, with the Home Office a little farther down. I don't suppose that the people in charge of any of those places would have approved much of what went on across the street at no. 4.

The way to get inside was the way that you get a lot of the other things you want in life – to know somebody. In May 1984 I had come to hear of some airborne radar equipment that I knew would be of interest to the Iranians. It was available for immediate delivery from Portugal. So I asked around my contacts until I found someone who had done deals with Victoria Street and I asked him how I should go about it.

He told me that the army, the navy and the air force had

separate buying departments at Victoria Street. For airborne radar I obviously had to contact the air force man and he gave me his name, Major Hammad. Without a name to quote you cannot get past the switchboard. I phoned and said I had some equipment that might be of interest to him. He wouldn't have expected me to say anything more on the telephone because if there was one certainty about that office it was that the security forces of nearly every significant country were plugged into the phones and listening in. I made an appointment to go and see Hammad.

On the door of the building was a crude, hand-drawn sign saying 'NIOC, 4 Victoria Street', with an emblem on it that I supposed was the trade mark of the oil company. Immediately beyond that door I went through a security check by a British guard from a private security service, including being scanned with a metal detector to stop anyone carrying in unauthorised weapons. I should have been surprised if there were not also a hidden camera recording everyone who entered and left: maybe several.

After the checks I came to a square reception desk where I gave the name of the person I wanted to see. They asked whether I had an appointment. If not – no chance. Then I sat in a waiting area furnished with plain light wooden furniture, upholstered in blue, a little scuffed and looking the worse for wear. A few Iranians were there as well – some of them no doubt keeping an eye on the comings and goings – plus the occasional British businessman out to make a fast killing. There was only one piece of decoration on the walls, and that appeared all over the building: a picture of Ayatollah Khomeini, Iran's spiritual leader, on whose behalf all this business was being negotiated.

On the tables were magazines in Farsi, the Iranian language. Nothing in English, but it didn't matter because I did not have to wait much longer than five minutes before someone came to take me to the third floor. The corridors all over the building were as sparsely decorated as the waiting area, with just as many Ayatollah photographs.

Major Hammad was, I would guess, in his mid-forties.

With him was a junior officer who said nothing throughout. I would get used to that in trying to do deals with Iranians. They all had their 'minders' because they did not want to put themselves into a position where they could be accused of accepting kickbacks from the transactions. In Victoria Street, almost alone among the great arms bazaars of the world, commissions were strictly forbidden, at least for those on the Iranian side. (Like the drinking regulations in much of the Arab world, exceptions may have been made in the case of foreigners.) The last thing they would do was risk anything that might get them sent home. I imagine that was the main dread of all of them.

These boys in Victoria Street were happy to be in London, and it was not too hard to understand why: there was no war going on here, no bombs dropping. They did not want to lose their positions and be forced to return to Iran and all its dangers, so the safest course was to take no risks and treat everyone with extreme caution. That is why I expect they were devastated when they had to leave in September 1987, although my guess is that the expulsion was followed by a rapid switch of oil company personnel, with military people being sent in to replace them and to carry on business as usual.

The three of us – Major Hammad, the minder and I – sat at a small conference table at the other end of the office from Hammad's desk. They offered me some of their national drink, sweetened condensed milk with hot water. I politely declined and did not tell them I should have preferred a gin-and-tonic, since all the evidence suggests they have no sense of humour. It soon became clear to me that, although Hammad was interested in what I was offering and the price – ten units at $115,000 each – we were going to have the usual difficulty over mutual trust and payment, the question of who pays whom first. Because he did not know me, Hammad wanted me to start the process by giving him a performance bond before he would supply me with a letter of credit. For the same reason, I wanted my LC first: and indeed I could not have secured the equipment from my supplier without it. But to look at it from their point of view, if they initiate an LC and *you* then don't perform, *they* have a problem. That is why they are so careful.

I suggested a pre-advised LC – an enforceable undertaking from their bank that if I issued a performance bond an LC would be opened. They would not do that and, after we had tossed proposals back and forth for around half an hour, it seemed that we could not surmount the problem. I went back to my office and explained the impasse to an Iranian I knew in London. Eventually he helped me get round the obstacle by putting his neck on the line. He assured Hammad that he had done business with me, that I was not a double-crosser and that he knew the equipment was available for delivery in Portugal.

Because the Iranians needed the radar equipment very badly, they finally accepted my friend's assurances and agreed to open a pre-advised LC with my bank, the Credit Lyonnais in Geneva. But they were still proceeding with caution. They inspected the stuff in Portugal but would not give the deal the final go-ahead until it was tested. The problem with this sort of gear is that the only way you can see whether it works is by taking it into the airborne radar units. So my LC was payable at only 50 per cent on delivery, the rest on acceptance.

It took about three months after our initial meeting before we were in a position to finalise the deal. The goods were shipped to Tehran three weeks after the agreement was signed, and integrated into the radar units. They duly worked and the Iranians paid up in full. Once deals are completed they are very good about paying. This is in distinct contrast to their enemies the Iraqis, whom I have traded with since – even though most of their weapons come from the Soviet bloc.

My second contact with Victoria Street came to nothing. I had some 155mm shells – 50,000 of them – available in Greece. These would have been for the army, and Major Hammad introduced me to his opposite number on the army side. But there was no sale. A country at war has to pick its priorities and at that time they had plenty of shells. But each failed deal teaches valuable lessons. I learned from that disappointment that I needed even better intelligence than I had about supplies my customers needed.

My commission on the radar deal was 10 per cent – or $15,000, the price of one of the ten units. This is not a fortune but I was pleased because it is hard to get a foot in the door and do business with the Iranians as a newcomer. Looking to the longer term, I thought that, because the goods had been delivered quickly and proved satisfactory, this would pave the way for other opportunities in what was the biggest market for arms at that moment. Both sides had behaved in a businesslike fashion and no law was being broken by either. No doubt our relationship would have developed and prospered had the Americans not decided secretly to reverse their policy and supply arms to Iran. Their move distorted the established market by threatening to cut out freelance dealers like me – unless we could get ourselves a piece of the Washington action.

The Americans had no reason to support either side in the Gulf war. The Iraqis were backed by the Soviet Union and were, as well, among the nations most virulently hostile to Israel, the United States' main ally in the region. As for Iran, quite apart from the agonies of the hostage issue, there was a growing conviction that many acts of terrorism in the Middle East, especially in Lebanon, were carried out with the knowledge of the Iranian regime, who might even have been giving active support to the bombers and kidnappers. In the aftermath of the hostage crisis, President Reagan had spoken out strongly against terrorism and set his face firmly against doing deals with terrorists, let alone supplying arms to them. The Americans' chief strategic interest was to see that, despite the fighting, the Straits of Hormuz remained open for US and other shipping.

Yet almost since the start of the Reagan presidency in 1981 there had been pressure from members of his administration for a review of policy on arms sales to Iran, initially from officials worried about the threat of increased Soviet influence in the Middle East. *The Chronology*, the day-by-day account, drawn up by the National Security Archive, of how policy towards Iran developed and led to the Iran/Contra scandal, shows that one of the first acts of Alexander Haig, Reagan's Secretary of State, was to approve the transfer from Israel to Iran of American spare parts for fighter planes that would have been inoperable without them. After that initial approval, deliveries appear to have been made with some frequency.

But supplying American equipment to Iran was against the declared official policy of the United States and, so long as it breached the arms embargo (if there was one), it was also against the law. From time to time the authorities would seek to reassert the law by bringing charges against people for defying it. In September 1982 Ian Smalley, a British arms dealer who lived in Texas, was charged with conspiring with two other men to sell Iran 100 M–48 tanks and 8300 TOW anti-tank missiles. (TOW stands for Tube-launched, Optically tracked, Wire-guided. It is a light-weight guided missile and launch tube suitable for the rugged country where the Iran/Iraq war is being fought. They are one of the prime weapons used in the war and the Iranians need them in large quantities.)

Smalley's arrest was the result of a customs 'sting' operation in some ways similar to the one that trapped me nearly four years later. Unfortunately I did not hear about it until far too late: otherwise I should have been forewarned. In February 1983 the Englishman was acquitted because the jury placed no credence on the evidence of the informer – not in this case Cyrus Hashemi but an arms dealer named Gary Howard. Part of Smalley's defence was that he had been persuaded to believe that the deal had US government approval.

In 1983 the State Department began Operation Staunch, a campaign to persuade other countries to comply with the US embargo against Iran. (If, as Poindexter later claimed, there was in fact no embargo, then the Americans were guilty of conning their allies, including Britain and Germany.) Operation Staunch was not, however, very successful, according to a report in *Time* magazine in July of that year. This revealed that American equipment worth hundreds of millions of dollars was sold to Iran every year through third countries and independent dealers. The report described in detail one such operation, involving a man I was to come to know three years later.

Cyrus and Balanian Hashemi, two Iranian brothers, had set up 'front' companies to carry out the trade in weapons. One company pretended to run Persian carpet shops in Stamford, Connecticut, and in London, while another, established by Cyrus Hashemi, was a general trading company called Zoomer Fly Ltd, also based in London. After this article appeared, the Hashemi brothers were tried and convicted of illegal arms dealing, although Cyrus was by that time safely in Britain.

Later in 1983 (although it was not revealed publicly until 1987) another company, unrelated to Hashemi's, was established to do arms deals with Iran. Its unusual feature was that it involved US government officials. According to a report in the *New York Times*, European Defense Associates was set up by Colonel Ralph Broman, who worked for the US Defense Department in Paris, and Paul Cutter, a diplomat who used to be attached to the CIA. The company had offices in the USA and Paris and attempted to sell arms worth hundreds of millions of dollars to Iran, including tanks, missiles, submarines and fighter planes. Also mentioned in this report were two names now familiar to me – Bernard Veillot, a French arms dealer who tried to procure some of the material for the Evans deal, and Manuchehr Ghorbanifar, the Iranian middleman who figured prominently in the inquiry into Oliver North's Iran/Contra operation.

In October 1983 the American embassy and Marine barracks in Beirut were attacked by terrorist bombs, and Iranian involvement was suspected. In January 1984 the US administration denounced Iran in strong terms as a sponsor of international terrorism, and toughened the arms embargo. A number of Americans and other nationals were later kidnapped in Beirut – again probably with Iran's complicity. One of them was William Buckley, the CIA head of station in the Lebanese capital. Colonel Oliver North, of the

National Security Council (NSC), tried to arrange a ransom for Buckley – who would eventually die in captivity. When that failed, the idea began to take shape in the NSC of swapping arms for hostages: the USA would allow some of its arms to go to Iran, either directly or through a third country, if its hostages were released.

The precise details are still disputed but it seems that Ghorbanifar (now thought to have been an Israeli agent) was the first to promote this exchange actively at a meeting in Hamburg in November 1984 with Theodore Shackley, a former CIA official. He argued that, apart from a possible hostage deal, to authorise arms supplies could strengthen moderate, pro-western influences on the Ayatollah. The US authorities reacted coolly to the suggestion at first, partly because they had known the voluble Ghorbanifar since the 1980 hostage crisis and were unimpressed with his ability to deliver what he promised. He was subjected to a polygraph test which found that he lied on a number of important points, including the extent of his contacts with the Iranian regime. Nevertheless, for want of any better intermediary, the Americans continued to use him. Meanwhile other Iranian middlemen were trying to bring off arms deals, either for cash or sometimes in exchange for sensitive information about Soviet influence on the Iranian regime.

In the summer of 1985 a CIA intelligence report gave a gloomy assessment of the prospects for US influence in Iran after the death of Khomeini. This prompted NSC strategists to compose a draft policy document proposing that allies of the United States – a clear reference to Israel – should be encouraged 'to help Iran meet its import requirements', adding: 'This includes provision of selected military equipment as determined on a case-by-case basis.' George Shultz, the Secretary of State, and Caspar Weinberger, Secretary of Defense, both opposed the suggestion, Weinberger in particularly forceful terms. But this did not deter North and his superior Robert McFarlane, the President's National Security Adviser, from pursuing it.

In a story full of oddballs and other unusual people, North is perhaps the most extraordinary of all. To me he represents a few of the best characteristics of Americans, but even more of the worst. A clean-cut colonel in the Marines, he was decorated for his bravery in Vietnam and spent much of his subsequent career running top-secret operations for the US security services. He is a decisive man with an extraordinary imagination. He would think up plots that seemed to come out of boys' adventure books. One elaborate scheme to free an American hostage in Beirut was said to involve paying a ransom in notes that had been treated chemically to disintegrate a few days after the payment. It did not go ahead and the hostage was murdered.

When he gave evidence before the Congressional hearings on Irangate, North portrayed himself as a super-patriot, totally honest and prepared to do anything for his country. This provoked an enthusiastic response from the American public, according to opinion polls, and there were even some who wanted him to run for President. But it was clear that he wanted to make his own decision on what was and what was not in his country's interests, even if it conflicted with the views of Congress and senior officials. His actions were dictated by his obsessive conviction that the United States had to help the anti-government guerrillas in Nicaragua in order to save the western hemisphere from Communism. Congress had refused to endorse such support on the scale requested by President Reagan, but this did not shake North's certainty that it had to be done.

He saw the arms sales to Iran primarily as a means to that end and placed little importance in the fact that both the Secretary of State and the Secretary of Defense were opposed to the course of action that he was undertaking, even though it fell right in their area of responsibility. If he thought it was right, he went on and did it regardless and quite unashamedly. In part of his testimony to Congress, he claimed that on one occasion, after details of the Iran/Contra deals became known, he had been shredding relevant documents while investigators from the Attorney-General's office were searching for evidence only a few yards away in his office.

His diversion of the substantial profits from the Iranian

arms deals (the Iranians were seriously overcharged) to helping the Contra guerrillas caused a bigger sensation when it was revealed than the deals themselves. I do not support the political line of the Nicaraguan government but I do not think that any other country has the right to give support to people trying to overthrow it – especially a country whose leader makes such a noise about denouncing terrorism. That is simple hypocrisy.

At the Congressional hearings, North made two points that had particular relevance to my case. Although he said that as far as he knew President Reagan had not been told about the diversion of funds to the Contras, he confirmed that the President had signed a document authorising the arms sales to Iran – and that he had done it before my alleged offences had been committed. North also said that Ed Meese, the Attorney-General, supported the plan to give the money to the Contras. Meese himself told the Congressional investigators on 28 July 1987 that Colonel North asked his view on secret sales of arms to Iran in January 1986 – three months before my arrest. Not only did he say then that he was in favour of them but he added his opinion that it was legitimate to conceal the sales from Congress. Yet as the country's chief law officer, Meese was ultimately responsible for bringing the criminal case against me and the others. If he knew North was doing the same as I was accused of, how does he justify the difference in treatment between us?

On 14 June 1985 the terrorist issue came to the fore again when a TWA aircraft flying from Athens to Rome was hijacked by two Shiite Moslems from Lebanon and forced to land at Beirut, where one American passenger was killed and thirteen others kidnapped. The kidnappers were supporters of Ayatollah Khomeini. The release of the hostages, after sixteen days, was a result of intervention by Hashemi Rafsanjani, the Speaker of the Iranian Parliament, after pressure from the US government. It was later disclosed that President Reagan sent Rafsanjani a message thanking him for his help, although a few days after the hostages' release the President made a speech denouncing Iran as part of 'a new, international version of Murder Incorporated'.

By now the Israelis were expressing interest in selling American arms to Iran with the permission of the US government and with a commitment that they would be replaced speedily by new American arms shipments to Israel. On 3 July David Kimche, the Director-General of the Israeli Foreign Ministry, raised the question with McFarlane at a meeting in the White House. Later that month Kimche went to Hamburg to discuss arms sales with Ghorbanifar, Kashoggi and others. Two Americans were also reported to have been at that meeting. They have not been positively identified but it is assumed they represented the NSC.

Kashoggi's role was to finance the Israeli/Iranian deals. This was necessary because neither the Israelis nor the Iranians trusted each other. The Tower Commission report explained it clearly. The Israelis gave Kashoggi the number of an account where the money for the arms had to be deposited, and Kashoggi made the payment. (He said later that he had borrowed the money from 'Tiny' Rowland.) The Israelis then set the supply in motion. Ghorbanifar gave Kashoggi a letter of credit, payable when the goods had been received and inspected in Iran. Kashoggi was simply the stakeholder, willing to trust both parties. I have often thought that if I could get someone like him to perform the same service for me, it would make a lot of my problems easier.

By August 1985 the outline of the deal was clear. The Iranians wanted 500 TOW missiles from Israel, and in turn undertook to release a hostage. (Buckley, the man the Americans wanted back most urgently because of his links with the CIA, had died in June, but this did not become known until October.) The arrangement was clearly approved at a high level in the White House, although whether the President knew at that early stage is still a matter of controversy. At the end of August, after elaborate transhipment arrangements were made through Portugal, involving a CIA-owned airline, the first 100 missiles were delivered. The Iranians, via Kashoggi, paid Israel $1 million for the shipment, substantially more than the Israelis had paid the Americans.

In September a further 408 TOWs were delivered and another $3 million changed hands. Two days later a single American hostage, the Rev. Benjamin Weir, was released from captivity in Beirut and allowed to return home. Some of the missiles, on inspection, were found to be defective and were replaced but both sides seemed reasonably satisfied with the deal.

Another dramatic terrorist incident grabbed the world's attention on 7 October 1985 when five Palestinians hijacked the Italian cruise ship, the *Achille Lauro*, off the coast of Egypt. One American passenger was killed and officials in Washington made the usual denunciations of international terrorism – while they were secretly doing deals with one of the countries supposedly backing the perpetrators. The hijackers surrendered after two days and were offered safe conduct in an Egyptian plane: but American fighters intercepted the aircraft and forced it to land in Sicily, where the hijackers were arrested by the Italian authorities. Two of the men responsible for this act of bravado were Colonel North and Vice-Admiral Poindexter. It was applauded by Americans and did a lot for President Reagan's popularity rating.

It did not, however, deflect Colonel North and his associates from going through with further arms-for-hostages negotiations with Iran. The next planned stage was the release of five remaining American hostages in return for a shipment from Israel of 120 HAWK surface-to-air missiles. The Iranians wanted these to ward off Soviet reconnaissance aircraft flying high – about 70,000 feet – over their border with the Soviet Union. But HAWKs, in their basic form, are effective only against low- or medium-altitude targets. The Iranians were disappointed with the first batch of eighteen, delivered in November, especially since they noted that they had Israeli markings.

Colonel North described their reaction in a note, written in early December, to Vice-Admiral Poindexter. 'This delivery has created an atmosphere of extraordinary distrust on the part of the Iranians,' he wrote, adding that Ghorbanifar had accused the Israelis and Iranians of playing 'a cheating game'.

To restore confidence, North outlined a proposed deal involving the supply of fifty upgraded HAWKs with a longer range, plus another 3300 TOWs. These would be delivered in stages, with one hostage released as each planeload of weapons reached Iran. As these plans became known to a wider circle of officials at the White House and in the CIA, some of them expressed concern about their obvious illegality. To keep on the right side of the law, they would have to be authorised by what is known as a presidential Finding, which gives the permission of the chief executive for a certain course of action to be taken in the national interest.

The wording of a Finding was drafted by a CIA official, including the sentence: 'Certain foreign material and munitions may be provided to the Government of Iran which is taking steps to facilitate the release of American hostages.' According to Poindexter at the Congressional hearings, President Reagan signed this Finding in December. Reagan also attended a meeting where the proposal was discussed, and where Shultz and Weinberger continued to oppose any trading of arms for hostages. Because of their opposition, that particular deal did not go ahead.

However, there were a number of people in the NSC who wanted to continue the attempt to release the hostages in return for authorising arms supplies. Ghorbanifar, too, was pressing for further action, stressing his argument that supplying arms would strengthen moderate elements in the Iranian armed forces by providing them with the prestige of winning the war against Iraq. This was reflected in a new draft Finding submitted to the President and signed by him on 6 January 1986. It contained the following passage:

The US Government will act to facilitate efforts by third parties and third countries to establish contact with moderate elements within and outside the Government of Iran by providing these elements with arms, equipment and related material in order to enhance the credibility of these elements in their effort to achieve a more pro-US government in Iran by demonstrating their ability to obtain requisite resources to defend their country against Iraq and intervention by the Soviet Union.

These were precisely the points I made in my statement to the court in June. I had not of course seen the draft Finding, but the similarity of my statement to it was clear evidence that the information on the secret American policy, as given to me and the others before we committed ourselves to the deal, was accurate. It shows not only that we were complying with American policy, but that we knew we were.

On 17 January 1986 President Reagan signed another, very similar Finding, but with one significant variation: Israel would no longer act as the channel for the military equipment. Instead, it would be supplied direct from the United States. The CIA would requisition 4000 TOW missiles from the Defense Department and transfer them to Iran. The President had thus authorised the direct sale of American arms for the first time since the embargo was imposed during the 1980 hostage crisis. As he noted tersely in his diary (obtained as evidence by the Tower Commission): 'I agreed to sell TOWS to Iran.' He was in fact giving the seal of his Presidential approval to the self-same offence that I was accused of three months later. The difference was that I spent seven months in prison while he remained comfortably established at the White House.

Now that the President had given the green light, North renewed his efforts to arrange further supplies of missiles to Iran. A new element of the deal was that the US would provide the Iranians with intelligence material about Iraq, as an extra encouragement for the release of hostages. There were also to be meetings between American and Iranian officials, one of which took place in Tehran and another in Frankfurt, both in February.

North and his associate Richard Secord were among the American representatives in Frankfurt. According to North's testimony at the Congressional hearing, that was the meeting at which Ghorbanifar, knowing of North's efforts to help the Contras, suggested that some of the surplus revenue from the Iranian supplies might be used to buy arms for the guerrillas. North said the suggestion had been made during a discussion in the bathroom of a hotel suite. This seemed so unlikely that many commentators did not believe it, but North insisted it was true. 'It was a neat idea,' he told the hearing.

That month Kashoggi provided a further $10 million bridging financing for the new Iranian deal, and deposited it in a designated account at Credit Suisse in Geneva. On 14 February the first 1000 TOW missiles were sent from the USA to Israel, which was still to be used as the transit point even though this new deal was a direct Iran/USA arrangement. They arrived in Iran a week later. (It was during these same early months of 1986 that Cyrus Hashemi was trying to trick me and the other defendants in my case into admitting in monitored phone calls that the arms we were trying to sell him came from America. He was trying to establish that an offence was being committed.)

The plan was that the American hostages should be released after that first delivery, then a further 3000 TOW missiles would follow. In addition, there would be more high-level meetings between American and Iranian officials in an attempt to improve relations between the two countries. But the Iranians upped the ante: they asked for another 500 missiles before the release. These were also delivered, but still no hostages came out.

In March 1986 the Iranians increased the stakes yet again: now they wanted some Phoenix air-to-air missiles to use with F–14 interceptor aircraft, and Harpoon missiles, to attack shipping. The American side refused to accept these new demands, and the deal was stalled throughout March. Ghorbanifar went back to Tehran and, on his return, had an all-night meeting with North and his associates in early April, at which the negotiations were resumed and a new timetable was drawn up, dovetailing the supply of new arms with the release of hostages.

An arrangement was made for Robert McFarlane, the recently retired National Security Adviser to the President, to visit Tehran, on a plane that would also carry some of the promised weapons. But there was clearly not much trust between the two sides and the Iranians continued to vacillate about whether they would release the hostages before some or all of the arms had been delivered. The Americans, for their part, were stalling about whether to include high-security radar equipment in the supplies.

During March tension increased in the Middle East when the Americans sent three aircraft carriers into the Gulf of Sidra, off Libya. The motive, it later emerged, was to provoke a reaction from Libya to justify a punitive US bombing raid. On 24 March the Libyans fired at the American ships and the Americans retaliated. Two Libyan ships were destroyed. Colonel Khaddafi, the Libyan leader, called for war with the United States but the incident did not immediately escalate.

However, on 4 April an American soldier was killed and others injured when a bomb destroyed La Belle discotheque in West Berlin. The Americans immediately blamed Libya, although later evidence showed that the Syrians were behind it. Ten days later American planes bombed Libya, inflicting severe damage on Tripoli and killing many people, including a girl reported to be Khaddafi's daughter. (Later evidence cast doubt on that.) One of the objects of the raid was later said to be to kill Khaddafi himself. This provoked further suspicion from the Iranians about United States goodwill in the arms-for-hostages deal. It also caused the death of one of the American hostages in Beirut, Peter Kilburn, murdered by his captors in retaliation for the raid.

By the end of the month no substantial progress had been achieved. Attempts to set up meetings between senior American and Iranian officials were constantly falling through at the last moment. The Americans decided that they would abort the project if no breakthrough was made in the next two or three weeks. At about this time Kashoggi approached 'Tiny' Rowland, the London businessman, to raise more money to finance the deal. Kashoggi assured Rowland that it had official backing and Israeli officials confirmed it. Still unsure, Rowland asked Charles Price, the

US Ambassador in London. Price said he knew nothing about it but checked back with Poindexter, who told him there were 'shreds of truth' in the assertion, but that Kashoggi's version was not wholly accurate. Rowland refused the request for more money. On 5 May North wrote in a memo to Poindexter, 'We do not believe that Tiny is still engaged in this effort.' Kashoggi eventually won promises of help from two Canadian businessmen. But by then I was enjoying the hospitality of the United States Department of Correction.

That was how US policy on arms sales to Iran developed, according to the report of the Tower Commission established at the end of 1986 to investigate the disclosures of the previous month, and in particular the role of the National Security Council (NSC). Further details came out in the Congressional hearings during the summer of 1987, when North gave evidence. But by the time all that material was public knowledge I had already served six and a half months in the Metropolitan Correction Center and was back in London on bail. At the time of my arrest in April 1986, hardly any of those details were known to me or to anyone else, although I did know the broad outline of the duplicitous American policy. So that the reader can understand the motives for doing what I did, it is important to set out the facts as I knew them at the time and as Sam Evans later fleshed them out. Some of the details in the following chapter conflict with the official version, particularly Sam's account of the role of Roy Furmark. Cyrus Hashemi, the key figure in the story from my point of view, rates only a passing mention in the Tower Commission report and was not named at all in the Congressional hearings, at least not in the published reports of them.

The exact truth of the affair may never be known. But what does emerge clearly from the next chapter is that Sam and some of his associates had excellent contacts inside the administration who were reporting the shifts of opinion in the NSC with an accuracy that could only have come from direct inside knowledge. Yet when I made those claims in court in New York, before the American arms deals with Iran became public knowledge, the prosecution poured scorn on them. It is not surprising they sought to discredit me and my co-defendants, because if we could show that what we were doing had the approval of the US administration, and we were aware of it at the time, we could not possibly be said to be engaged in deliberate criminal acts.

The New York District Attorney's office comes fairly low in the hierarchy of the Justice Department and I believe they genuinely did not know of the secret deals, although Edwin Meese obviously did. Meese said at the hearings that as late as November 1986, when the business was first revealed to the public, his inquiries into the sales of arms led him to conclude that 'there was no hint that criminal activity was in any way implicated in the Iranian transactions.' So I repeat the question: if it was not criminal for Oliver North to sell arms to Iran, how could it be criminal for me, Sam Evans and the rest to be doing it? Especially when we knew for certain – as our prosecutors (or should I call them persecutors?) apparently did not – that the policy had been approved at the very highest level of the United States administration.

4

Baiting the Trap

It was a damp, muggy morning in the first week of October 1985. I had driven early from home to the Cricklewood office and intended to spend the day seeing whether I could advance the biggest deal currently on my plate – selling two Canadian-made Buffalo aircraft to Sudan for $24 million. About half an hour after I got in, Sam Evans came on the phone. I was slightly surprised because I had not seen him for nearly two months. He wasted no time on pleasantries but came straight to the point.

'Hermann, I need to talk to you. Something's come up but I don't want to talk about it over the phone. Can you get down to Les A for lunch?'

I had not planned to go into the West End that day but I said I could get there if it was urgent. From his tone of voice, with its barely suppressed excitement, I guessed it was. Sam was one of the least hysterical and most collected men I knew. It had to be something big.

'Let's make it an early one,' he said. 'Meet me there at half past twelve.'

I arrived almost exactly on time and asked the doorman to park my Jaguar. The club does not open until midday and hardly anybody had arrived yet, but Sam was waiting at a table in the oak-panelled library. The steward quickly brought our drinks and then, for the first time, Sam told me about Cyrus Hashemi. Although his was a name I would not easily forget once I was allowed to know it, the discreet Sam did not identify him during this conversation or for some time afterwards. He referred to him merely as 'the Iranian buyer'. Even after I had begun negotiating with him, I was not allowed to know his real name. He asked me to call him simply 'the doctor'

Some time later, I discovered that Sam had met Hashemi early in 1985 through one of his clients, Roy Furmark, a New York businessman friendly with the late William Casey, then the Director of the Central Intelligence Agency (CIA). Furmark told Sam that he had learned from Casey something the lawyer found it hard to believe at the time: that the Americans had for some time been countenancing secret sales of arms to Iran. Furmark knew that Sam worked for Adnan Kashoggi and that the Saudi had been involved in arms trading. Furmark in turn was associated with Cyrus Hashemi, a wealthy Iranian banker and cousin of Hashemi Rafsanjani, the Speaker of the Iranian Parliament.

They had first come together as partners in a projected oil transaction. Hashemi had told Furmark that he had access to contracts for 100,000 barrels of Iranian oil a day. The idea was that this should be sold to a recognised oil brokerage, from where it would be sold on to one of the big oil companies. With the Iranian oil industry in some disorder ever since the fall of the Shah, that was the way deals were being done. The profit to Hashemi and Furmark was enormous – twenty cents a barrel, or $20,000 a day for as long as the oil kept coming.

Sam had done the legal work for their partnership. Now Furmark wanted him to introduce Hashemi to Kashoggi, with the idea that they could collaborate on lucrative arms deals. Sam had represented Kashoggi and his Triad Group for more than ten years but had never become involved in his arms business. In a deposition to the court in New York after his and my arrest, Sam said of Kashoggi's arms transactions:

> This particular activity was handled either by Mr Kashoggi alone, by Mr Kashoggi with the assistance of a few trusted Arab confidants or by Mr Kashoggi with the assistance of his marketing company – the latter, particularly in connection with the sale of defence equipment by Lockheed, Northrop and other American

defence contractors. The marketing company was a separate entity with its own staff including its own legal counsel (not myself) and I had no participation or involvement of any kind with that company or its activities.

Furmark introduced Sam to Hashemi. Sam, as he told me later, was immediately impressed by the Iranian's apparent wealth. His shirts were silk and so were some of his well-cut suits. His watches and jewellery were luxurious and opulent. Sam introduced him and Furmark to Kashoggi and in April 1985 they agreed to form a holding company called World Trade Group, with three specialised subsidiaries to do business with Iran: one to distribute farming equipment, one to trade in petroleum and the other to provide arms. Hashemi became chief executive of the group and Sam was appointed its legal counsel.

In June 1985 Kashoggi, Furmark, Hashemi and Sam went to Hamburg and met Manuchehr Ghorbanifar, an Iranian friend of Hashemi's who was to figure in the Irangate affair. The following month, according to Sam, Kashoggi and Hashemi went to Israel and met Shimon Peres, the Prime Minister, to discuss supplying American arms to Iran through Israel. (The Israelis have denied that this meeting took place.) Sam's impression then was that these sales would have the tacit approval of the United States government, even if they could not endorse them openly.

But soon Kashoggi and Hashemi fell out. Kashoggi was reported to have been going through financial difficulties at the time and perhaps could not raise the funds needed to fulfil his assigned role as the provider of the bankroll. This would not, however, square with the fact that, as we learned from the Tower Commission, Kashoggi and Ghorbanifar went back to Hamburg in July, without Hashemi, to discuss the arms prospects with David Kimche of the Israeli Foreign Office – one of the preliminary meetings for the Irangate deals.

In August Hashemi bought Kashoggi's shares in World Trade Group, although by then none of its three subsidiaries had completed any deals at all. A few weeks later Hashemi asked Sam to take part in the proposed arms deals not just for a legal fee but for 10 per cent of the action. They took offices for the operation in the Belgravia building where Sam had his law office.

Sam did not tell me any of these details when he summoned me to Les Ambassadeurs in October. But he did say that 'the Iranian buyer' was exploring the possibilities of procuring arms and wanted to know what might be available on the market. They wanted new arms made in the United States, and were already working on a scheme to ship some brand-new F–4E fighter planes direct from America. Sam assured me that the customer had a lot of influence on the Iranian government and he insisted that the deal would get American government approval. I had my doubts.

'Do you honestly believe that, Sam?' I asked him. 'I mean we all know that the Americans are selling arms to Iran through Israel, but you don't really believe that they would ship them direct from the US? There's still an arms embargo, don't forget. They hold Iran responsible for a lot of this terrorism in the Middle East. Think of the political embarrassment if it came out – and it would be sure to come out eventually. Our American friends aren't too good at keeping secrets.'

Sam then said something which at that stage I found totally incredible. It sounded like complete fantasy.

'The deal is by now on [Vice-President] George Bush's desk at the White House. It looks as if it's going to get the go-ahead.'

He told me his information came from two knowledgeable but mysterious Frenchmen he had met who had excellent contacts in Washington, probably with the CIA. Their names were John de la Rocque and Bernard Veillot. Their story was that the Americans wanted to do the deal precisely because they believed the Iranians had strong influence on the Lebanese terrorist groups who were holding several American hostages. Part of the package would be a meeting between American and Iranian delegations to discuss a resumption of normal relations between the two countries.

It was beginning to sound plausible but I was still not convinced. And although I am occasionally willing to cut corners and stretch the law to its limits to bring off deals, I did not relish the prospect of coming into conflict with the United States government. I reckoned that in such a contest I was likely to emerge the loser.

'Sam, I don't see any way you can get official approval for a deal like this,' I protested. 'If they want to sell that quantity of arms to Iran they'll have to do it either with second-hand equipment or through a third country. And if it's all so above-board why do they need middlemen like us?'

Sam explained that it had to be done covertly, through agents, so that the administration could deny knowledge if the truth ever became known. It was still possible that the obstacles to the deal would prevent it being completed and he wanted me to identify sources for second-hand fighters, preferably F–4Es, in case the new ones could not be procured from the States after all.

'Look around the market and see what you can lay your hands on,' he urged me. 'They want mainly American goods and they have two and a half billion dollars in the Chemical Bank in New York to fund the purchases. There'll be more if we show them we can perform.'

I nearly bit the top off my cigar. That was an enormous sum of money, even in a high-ticket business like military supplies. Between sips of Armagnac, I began working out my commission. When Sam suggested that he should arrange a meeting for me with the buyer, I leapt at the chance. I might not have been so keen had he told me one all-important fact about the Iranian. I don't think Sam was keeping it from me deliberately: he probably didn't know himself. Even if I had been allowed to know his name I would not have been aware of his past history, which I pieced together gradually from my researches much later: too much later.

In December 1979, according to documents obtained under the US Freedom of Information Act by the right-wing *Executive Intelligence Review*, Cyrus Hashemi proposed himself to the Carter administration as a mediator to obtain the release of the fifty-two Americans taken hostage in the US embassy in Tehran the previous month. One of the conditions of their release was to be the resumption of supplies of spare parts for American weapons in use by Iran's armed services. The secret deal was outlined in a memorandum sent to the State Department by Stanley Pottinger, the assistant Attorney-General, who had close links with Hashemi. It was never completed but in the course of it the FBI carried out a security check on Hashemi and tapped his phone.

That was how they discovered that he and his two brothers were arranging the supply of arms to Iran in breach of the US embargo. The arms, including rocket launchers and ground-to-air missiles, were shipped through Britain and Switzerland. Hashemi's bank, the First Gulf Bank and Trust, had helped handle the financial arrangements. In 1982 the three brothers and their associate Cyrus Davari were secretly indicted in an American court – but most of them had by then moved to London and only one of the brothers, Reza, was arrested in America. He was sentenced to imprisonment and warrants were issued for the arrest of the other two brothers and Davari, a former procurement officer for Iran in London. They could not be taken to court in Britain because the offence of illegal arms dealing is not covered by the extradition treaty between Britain and the United States – something for which I was later to feel relieved on my own account.

At the beginning of 1983 a Mafia-style murder took place in New York. The body of George Perry, an American businessman, was found attached to weights at the bottom of a lake in New York State. Perry was known to have been involved in Iranian arms deals with Hashemi. In August 1985, William von Raab, the US Customs Commissioner, said that Cyrus Hashemi was on the list of the ten most wanted arms dealers. In the circles I move in, that amounts to a first-class reference, so long as the person remains 'wanted' and stays out of reach of the authorities.

By this time Hashemi had already established the World Trade Group with Kashoggi and Furmark. Sam Evans had discussed the question of arms sales to Iran with a friend, Nicos Minardos, a colourful Greek-born actor who had played bit parts on television and now lived in California. Minardos had done business with Kashoggi before, which is how Sam came to know him. He introduced Sam to Veillot and de la Rocque, who told him that US arms sales to Iran were soon likely to receive official approval. Sam did not tell them that he had already been given that hint by Furmark.

Hashemi, too, had heard the same thing from Furmark but he was cautious enough to want to check it before going ahead with the deal. The stakes for him were high. If he were to fall foul of the American authorities again, his chance of ever being allowed back into America would disappear. So he asked his New York lawyer to make inquiries. When these drew a blank, Hashemi rethought his strategy.

There is no way of knowing exactly what he did next but the most common speculation is that he approached the US customs and offered to co-operate in laying a trap for Sam and the rest of us, in return for lenient treatment in the outstanding court case against him. It is on record that he pleaded not guilty to the arms charge and was released on bail of $100,000, with exceptionally liberal conditions: he was, for instance, allowed to travel freely outside America, where he could set up various arms deals with the connivance of the US customs.

But I have my own, different theory. I suspect that Hashemi's original deal was not with the customs service but with Colonel Oliver North or some other member of the White House group organising clandestine arms sales to Iran. Under the deal, I believe, Hashemi was allowed to roam the world trying, at the beginning, to do genuine arms deals for Iran with White House blessing. He had, after all, proposed the same thing six years earlier. There is support for this theory in a statement made by Elliott Richardson, President Carter's Attorney-General, in a British television interview in November 1986. He said that he had recommended Hashemi, a former legal client of his, to the CIA as a possible conduit for arms deals. Only when his activities began to get in the way of North's more lucrative deal, I believe, was it decided to abort Hashemi's operations and betray him to US customs, who then recruited him as the central figure in their sting.

Looking back, one maddening aspect of the affair, as far as I was concerned, is that for a long time it looked like proceeding without me. After that October meeting with Sam it seemed as though it would fall into that large category of deals that never reached completion, all talk and no substance. I looked around the weapons market and came across a package I thought would suit the Iranians perfectly. The Egyptian air force wanted to get rid of fifteen F–4E fighters. They had been made in 1971 and the Egyptians were switching to more modern equipment; but the Iranians use that type of plane and their logistics system is based on it. The planes were being sold as part of a package along with ten spare engines, a large number of spare parts, training equipment and 200 Sidewinder missiles to go with them.

From other sources I was able to get quotes for 30 M48 tanks, 140 engines for them (made under licence in Israel) and 15 Varion VA 145E amplifiers – part of the radar system used on F–4E fighters. The value of all the goods I offered was $320 million. I phoned Sam with the news and expected him to be enthusiastic, but I found him strangely cool. He said he would get back to me but he did not. I assumed that he was still working on the unlikely assumption that the Americans would approve the sale of the new planes. Much later I learned that he was pursuing those and other items through different agents, and he would only come back to me in a few months, when it seemed that his other potential sources, including Veillot and de la Rocque, had been unable to perform as promised.

Normally I would have been on the phone to Sam almost daily, urging him to let me supply the planes, but as it happened I had found another possible customer for them – or rather the same eventual customer, but through a different agent. Not long after my discussions with Sam I had been approached by a Spanish man living in London, who said he had friends in Israel interested in acquiring arms for Iran. We had preliminary discussions and a few days later, at the beginning of December, he introduced me to one of his Israeli contacts at the Royal Lancaster Hotel on Bayswater Road. Because I had not heard further from Sam about his project, I had no reservations about presenting the Spaniard and the Israeli with pro-forma invoices for the same Egyptian F–4Es I had mentioned to Sam over the phone.

The Israeli told me what I knew already – that Israel had been selling arms to Iran for several years now. But he added the extra information that many of the transactions had been set up by a man named Sam Hecht, an Israeli based in Zurich, who had business contacts with the United States as well as with Israel. (Too many Sams in this business, I thought to myself idly.)

'We suggest we go to Zurich together,' the Israeli told me. 'We can meet Hecht and discuss the business. If you can deliver, the prospects are extremely good. It is just a matter of getting the finance arranged and of getting the Iranians to issue a letter of credit.'

Yes, I reflected, it was always 'just a matter' of the financing – the heart of any deal, and the point at which they tend to collapse. All the same I knew that any ambitious arms dealer had to break into the biggest market at the moment, Iran. My radar equipment deal at Victoria Street had not opened the doors to me there in the way I had hoped: the military men were so tiresome to deal with, in any case. So I gladly accepted the invitation to Zurich and took John, my partner. With the Spaniard and the Israeli, we checked in at the Hilton. The first day we sat at the hotel waiting for something to happen, while our Israeli contact was on the phone constantly. Not until the very late afternoon did he announce that he had fixed a meeting for 8 p.m. in Hecht's office.

We took a taxi to the Olympia Centre, a modern office complex. Hecht's suite was on the ground floor. He was a man in his early forties, slim, tanned, with dark hair and wearing a dark-blue business suit. I noticed that his desk was piled with documents. Through a series of furtive glances, I was able to identify them as letters of credit from Iran for military equipment. In front of him he had copies of my proforma invoices for the planes and tanks.

Just before we started talking a man, clearly an Iranian, slipped in quietly and sat at one side of the room. He was not introduced and he said nothing throughout the meeting. His silent presence lent an air of mystery and conspiracy to the proceedings. I was told later that he was an Iranian official involved in arms procurement and wanted to keep an eye on any potential deals – playing the same role as the 'minders' at Victoria Street. I was also told that Hecht acted as an intermediary for many of the US/Israel/Iran arms deals and it wouldn't have surprised me to learn that he was connected with Mossad, the Israeli secret service.

He seemed pleased with my pro-forma invoices and said they would be forwarded to Iran. If the Iranians agreed to go ahead they would open a letter of credit with money they had available for this purpose at the Credit Suisse. At about 9.30 the meeting was over and the four of us went back for a drink in the bar of the Hilton. As usual, it was sprinkled with hookers but we did not take advantage of their offers of high-priced company. I, at least, did not need the stimulation because I was already preoccupied with the thought of the deal.

Next day we got up early and hired a Mercedes for the mountainous ninety-minute drive to Vaduz, capital of the tiny Alpine principality of Liechtenstein, where we had an appointment with a banker. It is always a problem to find banks able and willing to handle the unorthodox financial arrangements customary in the arms business. The amount of money involved is often so great that it deters bankers used to more mundane transactions.

Vaduz is a small town with two parallel main roads and a few cross-streets, filled chiefly with banks, restaurants and office buildings with hundreds of names on brass plates at the entrance, the registered offices of companies who have their headquarters there for tax reasons. We had lunch and went to the bank in the early afternoon. We had hoped that the bank would be able to handle all our end of this deal but, when he heard how much was involved, the officer in charge of foreign accounts shook his head sadly.

'My bank is not big enough to take accounts of this size,' he told us. So our drive, although it afforded picturesque views of snow-capped mountains, had been wasted as far as our business was concerned. We would have to try else-where. Next morning the Israeli flew to Israel and the other three of us returned to London to await developments.

I had not told my Spanish and Israeli contacts about the Sam Evans deal, so they were not to know that, a day or two before the Zurich trip, it suddenly surfaced again. Because it had been several weeks since I heard from Sam, I assumed something had gone wrong. But then he phoned and said it was time I met the Iranian buyer. He asked me to go to his Grosvenor Gardens office at around noon the following day. Two Iranians arrived at 12.15 but I was still not told their names. Seeing what time of day it was, I think they had expected lunch, because the first thing they said when they arrived was that they were hungry. Sam sent out for sandwiches.

The man I was later to identify as Hashemi was soft-spoken and seemingly a little shy, yet giving the unmistakable impression of power and opulence. He discussed the proposed deal in a matter-of-fact way, but was firm on one point: he was only interested in American material. The money at Chemical Bank had been earmarked by his principals for American goods and nothing else would be acceptable. Although I did not say anything, I thought it odd that he was so insistent on the matter. After all, when a country is fighting a war for its survival, and finds it hard to acquire arms by conventional means, it is scarcely in a position to be choosy as to their origins. Obviously they needed American spare parts for the equipment the US supplied in the days of the Shah: without them they would lose the war. But if they needed 155mm shells it surely did not matter where they came from. Greek ones, for instance, fit their guns and will kill as many people. And they are happy to use eastern-bloc missiles.

As it happened, I had been offered a piece of American

equipment a few days earlier, although it could not be classed as an instrument of war. It was a complete field hospital with 500 beds, fifteen years old but never used and with all the components still in their original packages. It would have cost $18 million to buy new but I could offer it for $2.5 million. Hashemi was dismissive, saying that he was interested only in hardware. But he did offer me a consolation: if I could provide him with the goods he was really after, he would agree to buy the field hospital as well.

I said I would scout around to see what I could come up with. He said he had people in America who would be glad to inspect the goods once I had told them where they were. That was much too much of a risk. I certainly was not going to give him the names of my sources because I did not know whether I could trust him. And even if I could, news of an inspection on American soil might leak out to people who did not know about the secret American policy.

'I don't think there'll be any need to go that far,' I said cautiously.

When the Iranians left I said to Sam, 'This guy seems a little strange.'

Sam replied, 'That's the way he is. I've known him for a few years and he's legit.'

'If you say so, that's fine,' I said. 'I'll get you the quotations and we'll see what happens.'

I prepared pro-forma invoices for the same planes, engines, tanks, ammunition and amplifiers I had offered to Sam Hecht. By the law of probabilities, as it operates in the arms trade, the prospect of just one of the two deals being completed was slight, let alone both of them. I charged the same price, $320 million, but added 15 per cent commission. The Iranian said he wanted 5 per cent and Sam 2 per cent, leaving me with 8 per cent, or $25 million. Even I, who have a hard head for money, trembled slightly at the tempting prospect. When I gave the invoices to Hashemi early in January, his eyes lit up and he too seemed greatly excited. He accepted the list and prices there and then, and wanted to do an immediate deal on the tank engines. He asked:

'Where are the goods so we can go and inspect them? My

people in America are waiting to look at them.'

'Hold on,' I cautioned him. 'That's not the way this business is done. First, I need from you a letter of credit or at least a proof of funds, a telex from your bank to mine.'

This seemed to disconcert Hashemi for a brief moment.

'You know we have set up a company, Galaxy Trade Incorporated, in New York to handle this deal, and we have half a billion dollars alone in our account at the Chemical Bank,' he said. 'I told you that already.'

'I know,' I said. 'But that doesn't amount to a proof of funds. That can only be done from your bank to my bank.'

That was the beginning of a long, sometimes farcical and finally fruitless chain of events, where I was trying to get confirmation that the funds existed and would be paid out for the goods I supplied, while Hashemi consistently refused to put anything on paper. I even made a phone call myself to David Faith, the vice-president of the Chemical Bank in New York, whose name Hashemi had given me. When I asked Faith why he would not send a proof of funds by telex he became evasive and said he could only speak to another banker. Faith, it later turned out, had been persuaded by customs officials to say that the phantom account existed, but the bank was too conscious of professional ethics – or the possibility of being caught – to put anything untrue on the written record. It is a strange professional code that allows you to tell lies, but only on the phone.

A day or two later Hashemi telephoned Sam in an attempt to overcome the stalemate. He told him how many millions of dollars' profit we might lose by being too fussy over the proof of funds.

'I think you're expected to make maybe $15 million in this deal,' he told him. Sam laughed.

Even had I wanted to, I could not proceed without a proper proof of funds. No supplier would agree to let me have weapons without hard evidence that they could be paid for. Another of my problems was that I had not yet identified a bank that would handle the transaction. Until I could find one, the deal could not go ahead, and I was having to stall Hashemi. My regular European bankers,

Credit Lyonnais in Geneva, would not do it. I went to
Liechtenstein again to try another bank there, but met the
same reluctance as the first time.

Back at my hotel in Vaduz, I decided to ring round all my
possible contacts until I found the name of a suitable bank.
The trouble was that the hotel was old-fashioned and had
no direct-dial phones. When the overworked switchboard
operator went off duty at 12.30 a.m., he switched the line
direct to my room. All the calls, as it happened, were for
me.

One of my contacts came up with the name of the Banque
Bruxelles Lambert in Brussels. Next morning I arranged an
appointment with them on the phone and flew from Zurich
to Brussels late that afternoon. While I was checking in at
the Brussels Hilton at about 8.30, Hashemi came on the
phone. I took the call in a booth near the reception desk. I
received many calls from him over the next few weeks and
they were nearly all characterised by bad connections. I
found it unusually difficult to hear what he was saying. It was
true that he had a soft voice but that would not explain the
crackling and interference, the occasional fading to unintel-
ligibility, which with today's technology should not occur on
a line between Brussels and London. Only later did I
discover the reason for this phenomenon – the calls were
being routed through New York, where they were being
monitored by customs agents. Looking back, those poor
connections were among the many circumstances that ought
to have made me more suspicious of the deal than I was.

Hashemi was still identifying himself over the phone as
'the doctor', and continued to do so even after he was aware
that I knew his name. It added a conspiratorial touch. On
this call the first thing he did was to scold me for having
made contact with Faith at Chemical Bank.

'He was quite upset that he had received a call from
somebody who was not a banker,' he told me. 'Now have
you got everything organised with your bank to call him?'

'That's why I'm in Brussels now,' I replied. 'Tomorrow
morning at 11.30 Belgian time, I'm going to be at my bank.
. . . They are very easy to do these things with, you know.'

Hashemi often got irritable on the phone if my arrangements seemed to be going slowly.

'You know we have already passed the names of two banks to New York,' he said angrily. 'I think that you must try definitely tomorrow to get the bank to call the Chemical Bank and, you know, resolve this matter.'

I repeated to him that I thought bankers preferred to do things on paper, via telexes, but Hashemi was adamant that a phone call would be sufficient. He was against 'everybody telexing back and forth' in a situation that he regarded as sensitive. He went on:

'Chemical Bank, you know, happens to be one of the largest banks in the world. The proof of the funds is for the bank to say that yes, the funds are here, we have the funds for this transaction, and in addition to the funds we have also a credit line which is non-utilised, for this transaction. That is proof of the funds.'

I told him that I would put that to the bank people when I saw them the next morning.

'I'm going to treat my bank manager to a big lunch afterwards and I will try and persuade him to phone the Chemical Bank in the afternoon, so that it's morning time in New York.'

Before he rang off, Hashemi raised two details, both of them embarrassing for me. He insisted that once I was satisfied that he had the funds, I should arrange immediate inspection of the tank engines by his agents in the United States. (I suppose, in the light of what happened later, these would have been customs agents.) And he asked, as he had done several times before, about the end-user certificates.

'I hope we are not going to have any problem as far as the EUCs are concerned, that you have them readily available.'

I was reassuring: 'Don't worry about the EUC. There's no problem.'

In fact there was a king-sized problem, in that I had no idea how to get end-user certificates that would come anywhere near passing the scrutiny of the US authorities. I had made no arrangements or inquiries on the subject, because Sam kept assuring me that the deal would get American approval, so it would not be necessary to do anything about false EUCs – or if I did have to get them it would be done with official connivance, so they would not have to be too convincing.

The question of inspection was if anything more tricky, because the tank engines were not in America and I was still not sure where they would be coming from. I had located supplies in Egypt and in Israel, from a factory that specialises in copying tank engines made elsewhere. Neither would be American-made, but since they were copies of an American engine I did not see why that should be a problem – as of course it would not have been if Hashemi genuinely wanted the goods, rather than to lay a trap for me.

I had not finalised the source because frankly I doubted whether the deal would come off and I did not want to waste my time. Arranging the actual supply was a hurdle that could be crossed later, when the question of the proof of funds was out of the way. Meanwhile, though, it was essential that I gave Hashemi the impression of absolute confidence and competence.

Next day I took a taxi to the Banque Bruxelles Lambert in Avenue Marnix, a classical, stately building with an ornate and impressive interior. I had made an appointment with Jean-Marie Dufays, the director for documentary credits. A smiling secretary showed me to a businesslike office where I met him, a pleasant man in his fifties. I took him to a small restaurant round the corner which he had recommended. Brussels has some of the finest restaurants in the world and we had a very good lunch. I told him the deal was for aircraft (without specifying the nature of the aircraft) and he was not put off by the size of the transaction. But he did say that the only correct way to verify funds was by telex. He would not phone the Chemical in New York for the proof.

'That is not the way we do things in banking,' he said. 'I am surprised that Chemical Bank think we should. I have no reason to phone them and I doubt that they would tell me anything over the telephone anyway.'

I went back to London where, at close to midnight,

Hashemi phoned again. I told him what Dufays had said and repeated that Chemical would have to send a telex. He exploded once more. He maintained that the same Brussels bank had in the past accepted proof of funds over the telephone, from a California bank smaller than Chemical:

'You're not calling a third-rate or a second-rate bank. They are calling, you know, one of the most important banks in the world. . . . There's absolutely no reason to believe that they would not release the necessary information to him.'

I suggested that to resolve the matter he could get his bank manager in New York to telephone Dufays. Hashemi agreed that this might be possible and I gave him the telephone number. Then we got down to discussing the details of the merchandise, in particular the thorny question of inspection. I was still assuring him that this could be arranged within four or five days of receiving satisfactory proof of funds from the bank, although I had no idea how I could swing it. I told him that I had been in touch with 'my people in the States' (who did not in fact exist) and that they would be coming to London the following week to get things moving. I also mentioned that they might be able to supply between twenty and fifty complete tanks, as well as the 200 engines.

I said I was aiming for delivery by early April. Hashemi seemed pleased by that and said he might well be interested in the extra items. It was an elaborate game. I was trying to keep his interest in me by enticing him with new items, which I could certainly have obtained but for which as yet I had no firm source in mind. Hashemi in turn was egging me on by giving encouraging though non-committal responses. It was like some bizarre courtship ritual. Once again, though, he brought up the thorny question of the end-user certificate.

'What EUC have you worked out now?'

'It is a NATO-country EUC,' I assured him lightly. I was making it up as I went along and proceeded to ice the cake: 'It is a prime and top EUC, but the moment we have your letter of credit in hand we have to make a division to a very, very high person. You understand?'

'Yes, yes,' said Hashemi.

I drove home what I was getting at: 'The division is not cheap, but it is going to work. You see, you always have two things in life. Either you get something cheap and you don't know if it's going to work, or you get something very expensive and it's going to work. The chap talks about five or six per cent – but he wants it, of course, guaranteed before he does it.'

Hashemi appeared to accept that, but then raised the question whether I and the suppliers could go to New York and meet him and his colleague who had to approve the deal, a man he said worked in the Iranian mission to the United Nations. As I did not want to go to the United States myself at that time, and as my colleagues in America were figments of my imagination, I discouraged the idea.

'My people would not open their faces at this moment,' I told him. 'Because you have to understand a deal like this is only possible when somebody right at the top is involved.'

Before the conversation ended I asked him what I called 'a little service'. Had he, I wondered, ever come across an Englishman named Brian Fodder?

'No, never,' he replied.

'If you ever do, be careful.'

'Why, who is he?'

'He's an English guy. He used to work for Scotland Yard at one time and he is now . . . er, playing around in our business . . . He is an informer.'

'Oh well,' said Hashemi quickly, 'don't let him get involved with us.'

'No, that's why I'm saying if you ever hear of this guy or if he ever gets in touch or anything, be careful.'

'Thank you for telling me. Obviously if I have something on our side I'll immediately let you know.'

That exchange was prompted by my continued uneasiness about Hashemi. I was still trying to weigh him up. I didn't trust him and I was trying to smoke him out by getting as much information from him as possible. I had found out that a man named Fodder was working as an undercover agent for the US authorities (I said Scotland Yard to mislead him). Some people had been arrested shipping electronic equipment from the USA illegally, as a result of Fodder's undercover work. If Hashemi had admitted to knowing him, my suspicions would have increased. But as he had not seemed to recognise the name, I felt slightly reassured.

Then I thought it was time to broach another question. Throughout all my dealings with him, neither Sam nor Hashemi himself had ever told me his name. But it was a very sensitive deal and I like to know who I'm dealing with. So I had phoned a contact at Victoria Street.

'Do you know a guy who calls himself "the doctor"?' I inquired, and described him.

'That sounds like Cyrus Hashemi,' my contact said.

'What do you know about him?' I asked.

'As far as I know, he's kosher,' he replied.

Thinking about it later, I supposed Hashemi wanted anonymity because it supported his image. Sam knew who he was and was aware of his indictment for arms offences but he was convinced that this deal was not illegal, because he had been assured that no shipment would take place before a meeting between a US and Iranian delegation. So he saw no harm in respecting Hashemi's wish not to be identified to the people Sam was dealing with.

At the very end of that January phone call I said to Hashemi: 'I never heard your name from you or Sam. I think it must be . . . something starting with an H.'

'Right, right,' he agreed.

'Can I mention your name on the phone?'

'Well I think, basically, if you call me in the mission in New York, just call me, you know, "the doctor".'

'The doctor,' I repeated.

'Right.'

The following week, on Thursday, 6 February, Hashemi phoned me at home at around 7.30 in the evening. I could tell he was very angry, from his reaction to my polite inquiry about his health.

'I'm not very fine,' he declared. 'In fact I'm a bit annoyed.'

He told me how David Faith from Chemical Bank had rung Dufays in Brussels, ready to reveal the details of the Galaxy account, but his call was greeted with indifference. Dufays pointed out that he had only met me once and I had not asked him to get any information. I had in fact already spoken to Dufays that afternoon. He gave me a slightly different version. He said that he had agreed with Faith that a proper proof of funds had to be by telex and not on the telephone. But Faith had said he had no instructions from his client to send a telex. There seemed no way to make progress.

Hashemi ranted on for a while about how reputable the Chemical Bank was and how it was ridiculous that the Belgian bank would not take their word about the sum of money that Galaxy had in the account. Then he threatened to break off the negotiations altogether:

'We have come to a point where I really have to know whether you will be able to provide us with these goods or if we're going to waste our time because obviously, you know, we have other options and I cannot, from the government's point of view, continue this process indefinitely.'

I felt I had to reply equally forcefully, to make him understand why I really did need something in writing. In doing so, I again embroidered the facts to a certain extent.

'Try and understand me, please,' I urged him. 'If I had the goods in my cellar I would be perfectly happy with a phone call from your bank. But please understand I am dealing here with a government. I am dealing with a very sensitive set-up and . . . I talked to the minister yesterday. He said: "Hermann, the only thing we want is a telex saying that funds of so much are available for the purchase." You see, the problem is for both sides really. I am stuck in the middle and so is Sam.'

Hashemi then switched tack. He picked up my point about my dealings with a government and recalled that I had said that the tank engines were actually in the United States. There could not therefore be another government involved in supplying them. Why couldn't I open a separate account with an American bank for the purchase of those, when everything could be handled through the American banking system?

I stalled and said I would talk to 'my people' and to Sam about it, and dangled the promise of further goods I could offer if we found a way to do this deal.

'I mean, I am not joking around or anything,' I assured him. 'I know the goods are there, I know the deal can be done. It's just a question of getting the first step so we can move on to the second step, which is my performance bond. And that's where we have to get within ten days, or a week if possible.'

Hashemi then turned to the subject of inspecting the engines, which he believed were in the United States. Why could that not be done 'immediately', he wondered, adding: 'We have the qualified inspectors.'

I had not yet decided how to break to him the news that the engines were not in America after all, so I tried another diversionary tactic. He was also interested in the Varion radar amplifiers. I suggested that we separated the two transactions and tried to make progress on the amplifiers, while leaving the tanks and tank engines in abeyance until we had sorted out the proof-of-funds issue. I had discussed that with Sam and he thought it a good idea. Hashemi was not keen, though. He said that he would lose credibility with his colleagues if, after having such a large sum of money tied up in New York for so long, he then only came up with a few radar amplifiers. Once or twice he said his 'head was on the line', implying that dreadful things would happen to him if the deal did not go through. But he took my suggestion on board, and later used it in his scheme to lure me to New York.

In another bid to satisfy the bank in Brussels, we had Sam Evans write a letter confirming that the Iranians had the money in the Chemical Bank in New York, but Dufays would accept nothing less than a telex from the bank. Hashemi then suggested that I or one of my associates in America could go to New York and visit the Chemical Bank in person. I was seriously thinking of going myself, that very evening, except that I could not get a visa in time. Hashemi then asked me whether I was dealing with the actual manufacturer of the engines. I said I could not explain it on the phone because I thought our conversations were being bugged: the previous evening a woman had phoned from the United States saying she was from the telephone company and asking who I had been talking to on Thursday evening. I did not give her any information but the call made me suspicious. Hashemi assured me that he was calling from the Iranian mission, which was entirely secure.

I was more and more convinced that the deal would not go through. Soon I would have to explain to Hashemi why he could not inspect the tank engines in America. I began proposing still more equipment he might buy. I had been offered 50 howitzers and 50,000 rounds of 155mm ammunition. Hashemi's first question, as always, was, 'Is it an American product?' It was Greek. No sale.

I did not go to New York the next day but had another talk with Hashemi over the phone. I had decided to confess that the engines were not where I said they had been. It was a difficult conversation.

'I haven't been very truthful to you from the beginning about the engines,' I said. 'They are not in the United States.'

'Well,' snapped Hashemi, 'where are they then? I mean, are they in Europe or what?'

'They are in Europe and they are manufactured in Europe under licence.'

When Hashemi began to repeat that he was not authorised to buy non-American goods, I argued that since they were made under licence from an American company, it came to the same thing. It did not, of course, come to the same thing for Hashemi, who needed me to be conspiring to sell American goods to establish an offence with the American authorities. He phoned Sam the following day and said he was 'boiling with anger' about my subterfuge over the tank engines.

'I don't believe anything he says,' he told Sam. 'I have no confidence in him and I think that, you know, he's probably trying to have a con game here.'

After that we had no more contact for two months. In truth, I was quite relieved. I felt I had maybe been a bit too clever, had got too deeply enmired in committing myself to something I could not perform – at least not in the odd way that Hashemi wanted me to perform it. The prospect of my multi-million dollar commission was alluring, and it was painful to see it vanish into the distance beyond my grasp; but on the other hand it was precisely because the stakes were so high that the deal had always seemed something of a long shot. I had other customers – less lucrative, for sure, but also less difficult to pin down. So I made no attempt to approach Hashemi to get things moving again.

Had I known about Hashemi's other contacts with arms dealers during this period and earlier, I should have stayed well clear of him for good. Sam knew a bit more than I did but, being a lawyer, he is trained in absolute discretion, and never gave me any more information than I strictly needed – the same reason why he kept me in the dark about Hashemi's name for so long. But even Sam did not know about the scores of conversations the Iranian was having with other suppliers – all, as it turned out, being taped by the customs service. In them, Hashemi laid constant stress on three aspects – the prime importance of the equipment being American, the impossibility of the deals being approved by the United States government and the need to get false end-user certificates.

His reasons were these: it is not an offence in America to sell non-American arms and naturally it would not be an offence to do anything that had government sanction; and to supply false EUCs would amount to an attempt to defraud the authorities. He raised the EUC question in at least thirty-six phone calls between January and April, but, despite that, none of the dealers, including myself, ever produced a certificate for him. I was not involved in most of these conversations and learned about them only from the court proceedings, but they illustrate the nature and scope of the 'sting' operation that trapped me and the others.

On 3 December Sam and Hashemi had gone to the Hotel Raphael in Paris to meet Veillot and a man and woman who were said to be from French intelligence. Hashemi was wearing a microphone to record the meeting for the US authorities, although the resulting tapes were hard to decipher. Veillot repeated his claim that Iranian arms deals were now being approved in Washington, naming as his source General P. X. Kelley, Commandant of the US Marine Corps, said to have been a schoolfriend of Veillot's associate, de la Rocque (who was not at the meeting). Kelley, according to Veillot, had been given the information by Caspar Weinberger, the Secretary of Defense.

From this point onwards, Hashemi's telephone calls were taped by customs officers. In many of the early ones he sought to disabuse the arms suppliers of the idea that the deals would get official approval. In the first taped call, on 9 December, Sam told Hashemi that US approval would not be announced officially, but 'the approval has to be there or it's not going to happen'. He went on, 'Unless the whole thing's a fairy tale . . . it has to represent government policy, at an unofficial level.'

In the ensuing days Hashemi made several calls to Veillot, who had undertaken to arrange the supply of a large quantity of arms including thirty-nine unused F–4E fighters said to be crated for delivery in America. In a conversation on 17 December, Veillot went so far as to say that he had been speaking personally to Weinberger, who assured him that the decision on approving the sales was now in his hands. He also indicated that, in return for this official authorisation, the Iranians were being asked to enter into talks to improve relations between the two countries, and to show their good faith by giving the Americans the serial number of a Russian-made tank captured from the Iraqis, plus the names of Russians attending a meeting in Tehran. By the end of December Evans and Veillot were assuring Hashemi that documents approving the deal were on Vice-President George Bush's desk, waiting to be signed.

Hashemi clearly did not believe that any approval would be forthcoming. Nor did it serve his purpose to have his suppliers constantly referring to the prospect in tape-recorded conversations. It made it harder for the authorities to contend that it was our intention to do something illegal. So Hashemi arranged a further meeting at the Raphael in Paris on 7 January, taking with him two special agents from the US customs, Joseph King and Ed Romeo. Hashemi introduced them as retired intelligence agents who knew about American policy. As soon as Veillot started talking about the deal being on George Bush's desk, King and Romeo said this was not true and that the only way the deal could be done was by breaking the law and by obtaining fake end-user certificates. They called this option two, option one being the above-board method, which they said was impractical. Despite this apparently authoritative guidance, Veillot continued to insist that his sources were highly reliable and that option one stayed very much alive.

It is still not clear exactly who Veillot and de la Rocque were and what links they had with the White House. My conviction that they were genuine US intelligence agents seems confirmed by the way they have gone to ground since our arrest in New York and have never given their side of the story. They were named in some of the early indictments against us but not in the later ones. They identified themselves with US diplomatic passports. I think they worked for the National Security Agency in a covert operation to supply Iran with arms as part of the secret US initiative.

The two men were obviously knowledgeable about what was going on in Washington, because the Tower Commission report showed that on the same day as that Paris meeting, 7 January, President Reagan had an eighty-minute meeting with Bush, Weinberger, Shultz and other senior advisers, to discuss overtures towards Iran, and they agreed by a narrow majority to go ahead with them. A few days later the sale of the first 1000 TOW missiles to Iran was authorised.

In his almost daily telephone calls to Sam and the others over the next few weeks, Hashemi persisted in expressing his doubts about Veillot's story, and in pushing for the illegal option two.

'We want to get these things shipped,' he told Sam the day after the Paris meeting. 'Otherwise there'll be no credibility left.'

But the suppliers were still banking on option one, being most unwilling to break the law unless there was absolutely no alternative. When Sam again said he thought the official approval was imminent, Hashemi responded:

'You know and I know up to now that it's not sanctioned, and it's not approved, and I honestly don't think from the way they explained it to us they are ever going to get the approval. The question is really, you know, are they going to be able to deliver or not? You know, we have been getting a run-around.'

Next day he called Sam again and asked specifically about obtaining a false end-user certificate. And the day after that he was on to Veillot, who told him that not all the goods being discussed could be obtained via option two, which would anyway be much more expensive than option one. He did, however, mention the possibility of obtaining an end-user certificate from a country in South America.

Veillot also backed down at this point on the thirty-nine F–4E fighters. There might now, he said, be only ten to thirteen of them available. He said he could get French Mirage jets to fill the gap but Hashemi turned them down, explaining again that he was not authorised to buy anything but American equipment.

By the end of January Sam was conceding to Hashemi that official, on-record US approval for the deal was unlikely, but 'they are willing to let it go ahead on an EUC basis, which of course they know is an arranged EUC.' Hashemi now became more insistent that the deal would be unofficial. He quoted his 'intelligence contacts' Joe and Ed (King and Romeo, the pair he had taken to Paris) as saying 'absolutely and categorically' that no government approval would be obtained. He urged Sam to go ahead with option two 'and not, you know, tell us stories about US government approval, which is not true'. And he began to give veiled warnings about what could happen to them both if the goods were not in the end supplied:

'I'm on the line, you're on the line,' he said. And two days later he was angrily urging Sam not to give him 'the same kind of bullshit' but to 'show me the end-user certificate'. Although the tapes show that Sam became ever more nervous about raising the subject of official approval with Hashemi, through fear of provoking similar outbursts, he was still getting persistent and convincing reports from de la Rocque and Veillot about the accommodating mood in the White House. On 7 February they revealed with precision the line-up among senior officials: George Bush was in favour of opening up arms sales to Iran while Shultz was against it, 'but nevertheless they are willing to proceed.' In fact, President Reagan had already, on 17 January, signed a document authorising the sale of the 4000 TOW missiles.

By now Hashemi was showing more and more anger in his phone calls to the dealers. On 7 February he ranted at Veillot:

'We have been dealing with you for two and a half months and frankly I'm annoyed, embarrassed and very un-happy. . . . If you've got the products, if you've got the goods, I don't care how you're going to get it, give it to us. We're willing to pay more than normal for the end-user certificate and, for Christ's sake, enough is enough. . . . Get these materials to us and let's move it.'

Veillot refused to be provoked by this outburst and pointed out that, if option one came about, it would have a beneficial effect on relations between the United States and Iran in the long term. Minardos, too, was reporting in similar optimistic terms, based on his own contacts in the administration. (He was friendly with Maxwell Rabb, US Ambassador in Rome.)

By February Hashemi was established in New York, having squared himself with the authorities over the out-standing arms-smuggling case against him. He occupied a suite at the Beekman Tower, where the customs service had placed hidden video cameras and microphones. Sam and Minardos went to see him there and continued to discuss possible US approval of the deal, despite the fact that the subject clearly enraged Hashemi. Much of the equipment was going to come from Israel, and Minardos said:

'We don't want to do something straight-out illegal, Cyrus. I personally don't believe that the Ministry of Defence in Israel is going to make this kind of a sale without checking with "Momma". I'm positive that the US government is pretty much aware of what's going to happen.' Four men from Israel were arrested with Sam in Bermuda on the day I was arrested in New York. They included Avraham Bar-Am, a retired Israeli general. One of the Israelis, William Northrop, had early on sought to arrange for the release of four Israeli prisoners in Lebanon as part of the deal.

On the question of the origin of the arms, it turned out that I was not the only person who had been less than exactly truthful to Hashemi about whether they came from America. Early in April Albert Flearmoy, the small-time British dealer arrested in New York on the same day that I was, tried to persuade Hashemi to accept British Swingfire missiles instead of the American equivalents. When Hashemi pointed out that by his contract he had to supply American goods, Flearmoy said that he could easily describe them as such if that would satisfy the people Hashemi was dealing with. Hashemi told him not to do that. 'I can't play with my government,' he said. All the same, Flearmoy was persuaded to go to New York on 21 April. When he arrived there he confessed that he had no American arms to sell, and doubted whether Hashemi would get any because of government restrictions. 'People dare not move American equipment at the present moment,' he explained. The idea that the US authorities would be fooled by false EUCs, without going to the trouble of checking them, was ridiculous to anyone who knew the first thing about how these matters work.

After Hashemi broke contact with me in February, I continued work on my other deals – the Buffalo aircraft for Sudan, screening smoke for Oman, machine guns and mine detectors for Chile, plus ration packs and tents for the

Chilean Antarctic project. (The problem here was to raise finance, because Chile's credit rating is not the greatest.) Through my earlier contact with Sam Hecht, I was making good progress on the sale to Iran of 1000 Milan anti-tank missiles – a popular weapon jointly developed by Britain, France and Germany. The deal was near completion and I had spent three days in Marbella in mid-April, staying at the Beach Club, to settle the final details and sign the papers.

I returned from that trip on Thursday, 17 April, to hear from my secretary and from Noi that Hashemi had been bombarding my home and my office with telephone calls. On my first night back he phoned at about 10.30.

'I haven't heard from you for some time,' he began. 'I was wondering what was happening.' I responded that I had wondered why I had not heard from him, but he did not waste time on explanations. Instead he came out with a firm proposal to break the logjam over the proof of funds. It involved my going to New York as soon as I could. There Hashemi and his colleague would give me a cash payment of $115,000 for one of the Varion amplifiers, plus a letter of credit for the remaining fourteen, payable when the first one was delivered. It was an attractive lure. I would actually get my hands on some cash. The trouble was that I was due to go to Portugal at the weekend to arrange for inspection of the Milan missiles in the other deal. Portugal is a popular place for the storage of military material because Lisbon is a free port and the arms stay in bonded warehouses. Customers can inspect them in the warehouses prior to shipment. After Lisbon, I planned to return to Zurich to complete the business.

I asked Hashemi whether the New York visit could wait a week. He said it could not, because the money on deposit in the Chemical Bank would have to be repatriated to Iran by the following Wednesday if it had not been disbursed. I asked why the business could not be done in London, where we were both based. He replied that his co-signatory could not leave New York because of his diplomatic duties at the United Nations. He was keen to meet me in person, because of the problems there had been, to resolve any lingering doubts about my bona fides. They were offering me a letter of credit that I would not have to match with a performance bond.

'The least you can do is to come and sign an agreement,' Hashemi pleaded. To sugar the pill still further, he spoke of possible further deals on other equipment. I explained that my Portuguese trip had been arranged for some time, but asked him to telephone me the following day at home.

It was certainly a cause for suspicion that Hashemi had contacted me again after an interval of nearly ten weeks, but when you have been dealing with the Iranians for some time you learn to expect the unexpected. I immediately phoned Sam for guidance, and he told me that Hashemi was already in trouble in Iran because an earlier deal he'd started had come to nothing. He was therefore especially keen to get some arms for his country before the funds at the Chemical Bank were repatriated the following week. Sam told me that he was arranging with a group of Israeli suppliers to go and sign a deal with Hashemi, although they were going to meet up in Bermuda because the Israelis thought it would be diplomatically embarrassing to sign the deal in the United States, where it was still technically against the law. Sam and I assumed that, after all the arguments about payment, Hashemi had finally persuaded his colleague to agree to pay me some money on trust, because the situation was so urgent and so desperate. But I was still undecided.

When Hashemi called next evening he asked straight-away, 'Have you made arrangements to come?'

'I have a problem,' I insisted. 'I have to go to Portugal on Monday.'

'If you aren't able to come,' he replied, 'regretfully we have to forget about it.'

I had a thought. 'Would you accept if I sent my business partner?'

John Saunders was still my partner although I was getting disenchanted with him and was looking for ways of untangling myself from the partnership. Hashemi hesitated slightly and then said he would be acceptable.

'I will talk to him tonight,' I said. 'He's just got back from Beirut.'

'Maybe you can send him to Portugal,' Hashemi suggested, 'and you can come to New York?'

'One of us will come,' I promised him. 'Okay?'

'It will take only one or two days, that's it,' Hashemi assured me earnestly.

That evening I was having a drink with an old and reliable friend. I mentioned my proposed trip to New York.

'I feel very funny about this deal,' I confided. 'It's been going for some time and I have a gut feeling about it.'

'If that's the case I wouldn't go,' said my friend. I said I would think about it.

Hashemi phoned me at home again on Sunday evening. I told him that either John or I would definitely go to New York, and I would look up the flights as soon as I got to the office the next day. I assured him that John was reliable.

'I've known him for six years. He's my full business partner,' I said. 'But when one of us comes, we don't want to come for nothing.'

He again outlined the arrangement – a cash advance for one amplifier and a letter of credit for fourteen.

'We will trust you on delivering the first one,' he said. Then, in case I still needed urging, he reminded me: 'By Thursday, the end of the Iranian week, all the funds will have been transferred and the transaction is closed.'

'We'll talk tomorrow,' I said, 'either personally or on the phone. But I'll have to leave on Tuesday.'

'You can be in London on Wednesday morning,' he reassured me. 'I'll phone your office to find out your flight. We'll pick you up at the airport and reserve a hotel room for you.'

I could not persuade John to make the trip. When Hashemi phoned at midday on Monday, my instinct was still to stall and I told him that I had decided to postpone it until Tuesday. I had booked on a plane that left London at 11 a.m. and arrived in New York at 12.30.

'That's going to make it very close,' Hashemi observed, pointing out that by the time I arrived in the city it would be quite near to the banks' closing time. I said there was a flight at 6.30 that evening that I might be able to get.

'That will be much better,' he said. 'Then you can have a good night's sleep and we can do the business in the morning.'

'Just make sure everything is prepared because I will have to leave again tomorrow,' I reminded him. 'I'll phone you at 4 p.m. my time and let you know what time I'm arriving. I'll try to make it tonight.'

I had finally made a firm decision to go. I was determined to satisfy myself once and for all whether or not Hashemi could perform. I wanted to see that the money and the LC were available in the bank. I further decided that, tempting though it would be, I would not actually receive the money or the LC while I was in New York, so no offence would be committed on American soil. Instead, I would have them transferred to my Belgian bank. I thought that would put paid to any set-up. I had not realised that in America, unlike in most countries, tape recordings can be used as evidence, nor that there is a charge of conspiracy that means they can get you for just talking about doing something, even if you do not actually do it. I should have taken some sound advice from an American lawyer before I left.

As I was on the point of leaving the office to drive to the airport, I did something quite out of character. I unloaded everything of significance from my briefcase, relating to other deals. There was scarcely anything left in it except my book of telephone numbers. Then I drove to Terminal 4 at Heathrow and put my car in the short-stay car park.

5

The Prisoner of Foley Square

The trouble with American law-enforcement officers is that they watch too many movies. They think they all have to act tough and mean, like Sylvester Stallone. They don't talk to their prisoners, they shout at them, in that tense, excited tone of voice that cops use on television when they are holding a revolver at arm's length and warning their victims not to move. The people from the customs department who arrested me were obviously enjoying it, particularly one called Dennis Doyle who, I learned later, had done most of the groundwork, including the telephone taps, under the overall command of Joe King. The woman who had been organising things after my arrest had not been involved in the investigation.

They do everything according to a fixed pattern. After they took me from the Beekman Tower bar to my room, the woman told me I had the constitutional right to remain silent. Doyle's eyes fell on my expensive grey briefcase. He eagerly picked it up and rummaged through the contents. I don't know much about American law but I was fairly sure he ought not to have done that without a search warrant. Still, there was no point in complaining at that moment, when I was clearly powerless to stop him. And it gave me a crumb of satisfaction to see his face fall as he examined the contents. All he found was a few old hotel bills, some stationery, my air ticket and book of telephone numbers. No contracts or invoices, and above all no end-user certificates.

I was right about the need for a warrant and to put matters straight Doyle applied for one retrospectively, a few days *after* he had made the search. The warrant said they were looking for 'evidence and instrumentalities of the crime of conspiracy to sell American arms to Iran . . . including documents relating to shipping, equipment specifications and his travel arrangements, as well as contracts, pro-forma invoices, end-user certificates, letters of credit and address books and deposits'. By the time it was drawn up, though, they already knew they had not found anything incriminating.

When we arrived at the Customs House at the World Trade Center, I had my photograph and fingerprints taken. Then we went to a conference room on the fifth floor, where the woman read me my rights again and made me sign a form whose words were once more familiar from the movies:

'You have the right to remain silent.

'Anything you say can be used against you in court, or other proceedings.

'You have the right to talk to a lawyer for advice before we question you and to have him with you during questioning.'

Underneath that was a waiver: 'I do not want a lawyer at this time. I understand and know what I am doing. No promises or threats have been made to me and no pressure or force of any kind has been used against me. I hereby voluntarily and intentionally waive my rights and I am willing to make a statement and answer questions.'

Although I was bewildered and upset, I had my wits about me sufficiently to realise that I ought not to sign that. No way. This meant that questioning was restricted to what the woman, in another strange piece of jargon, called 'pedigree information', as though I was a racehorse. They asked for my address, my former address, names of my parents, my brother and sister, identifying marks, height, colour of eyes and hair, employment record, address of bank – everything.

It was past 1 a.m. by the time they took me back to the car, still handcuffed, and drove me to the office of the federal prosecutor, where I had my first encounter with Lorna Schofield, the woman who was to blight my life for the next six and a half months. After a few more formalities I was taken to the place that would be my home for that period, the Metropolitan Correction Center (MCC), a modern remand prison adjoining the federal court house and New York's main police station.

They took my fingerprints and picture again and put me in what they called a holding cell on the third floor. It was a bare room, empty except for a concrete bench, covered in plastic, that went all the way round. I was kept there until around 5 a.m., when I was taken to a narrow, wedge-shaped small room with a folding sun-bed. Naturally, I was in no mental condition to sleep. After only an hour and a half they put me back in the holding cell.

Now people started coming in. There was a group of Italians that I guessed immediately had something to do with the Mafia. Then three more men came and sat on the bench directly opposite me, followed by a Dutchman who found room next to me. It turned out he spoke German and we started talking.

After all that had happened, and being short of sleep into the bargain, I was not in the best frame of mind to begin with – and the conversation did not make me feel any better. The Dutchman said he was there because he had sold some American military trucks and had already spent eight months awaiting trial. Eight months? I was determined to get out in eight days – eight hours if possible. I stood up, then paced back and forth across the room.

When I reached the other side I noticed that the three men on the bench, who looked as distressed as I was, were talking in English. But they did not look like Americans – except for one, wearing a rather battered silk suit. I heard him mention the name Sam.

'Hang on,' I thought to myself. 'Sam . . . I wonder.' I walked back towards them.

'Excuse me,' I said. 'I just heard you mention the name Sam. You don't by any chance mean Sam Evans?'

They looked at me as if I were a ghost.

'You as well?' said one.

'That's the way it looks,' I replied. And that was how I first clapped eyes on three of my alleged 'co-conspirators' – Ralph Kopka, Albert Flearmoy (who liked to be called

Larry) and Nicos Minardos. It was also when I realised for the first time how many other people Hashemi and the customs service had caught in their trap. The nightmare of the last twelve hours was beginning to make some kind of ominous sense.

I joined them on their bench and we swapped our experiences. Like me, they had all been arrested the previous day after being lured to New York by Hashemi: flies to a fly-trap. Kopka and Flearmoy had arrived together from London. Flearmoy was the eldest of the group, a big-talking Englishman in his sixties who had been involved in some low-grade arms deals with Rhodesia at the time when Britain was imposing sanctions on the white regime there. He had not been actively involved in the weapons business for some time, and made his money from a clutch of other entrepreneurial activities, including the ownership of a chain of hairdressers called Barbarella. He appeared to have joined Evans' group of suppliers as much for the adventure as from any realistic prospect that he would be able to supply any of the goods the Iranians wanted. More than most people in the business, his tongue had run way ahead of his ability to perform – and careless talk had cost him his freedom.

Kopka had a business connection with Flearmoy. A German in his early fifties, he had been sales manager of a truck company but retired early because of his health. He was an expert in contracts and Flearmoy had brought him to advise on the contractual side in case any deal came to fruition.

As I had been, the two men were met at Kennedy airport by a man who said he was Hashemi's driver, and taken to the Beekman Tower to meet the Iranian. After their meeting – like mine, secretly recorded on video – they were told that rooms had been booked at the Vista Hotel in the World Trade Center (conveniently close to the Customs House). Instead of drawing up to the hotel entrance, though, the car swung into the underground car park beneath the Customs House, where the pair were arrested.

Minardos was the most attractive and most talkative of the

trio. A tall, tanned, handsome Greek-born extrovert, now living in Beverley Hills, California, he had once been an actor playing bit parts in television serials. (He is a conceited man, and one of the aspects of the case that most offended him was that the American newspapers persisted in calling him a 'small-time actor'.) He had been brought in by Sam because he had once done some dealing for Kashoggi. He is a pleasant person, of the sort I call a party guy; he gets invited to a lot of parties. He acted as a fixer for Kashoggi. He is not an arms dealer but, like the others, was tempted by the lure of a fat commission.

Had I known that people like him, Flearmoy and Kopka were involved – essentially amateurs – I should have steered well clear of the whole deal. I discovered later that they had all had their air fares paid by Hashemi, in other words by the customs service. (They did not offer to pay mine because they must have known I would not have accepted. Can you imagine going to do a $320 million deal and not being able to afford a first-class air ticket?)

Minardos was only in transit through New York. He was planning to go on to Bermuda where, as Sam had told me before I left London, a meeting was scheduled with a group of Israelis who were going to provide more arms for Hashemi. Bermuda had been chosen as neutral ground, only a couple of hours' flying time from New York. I learned later that it was not just a question of diplomacy that had made the Israelis steer clear of New York: some of them feared that the deal might be illegal, despite the assurances Sam had from Veillot and de la Rocque, and from the mysterious 'associate' of Hashemi who turned out to be Joe King.

Minardos had played a role in the Israeli side of the deal and was going to Bermuda to join the others. He stopped in New York to meet Hashemi and was due to take his onward flight in a private plane. He went to Beekman Tower, had his meeting with Hashemi and then climbed into the car that he thought was taking him to the airport. Instead it took him to the car park of the Customs House, where he too was arrested.

We sat talking for maybe a couple of hours before we

were taken before the magistrate to be formally charged. The federal court house is an imposing building with wide steps leading up to a row of sturdy pillars in front of the doors. Getting there from the prison involved a complicated routine – but not as complicated as the one I would become familiar with after I became a fully-fledged prisoner. On that first day we were handcuffed and taken to a side door of the prison. Beyond it was a huge steel door attended by a large black guard with a .45 pistol slung on his belt. Inside the prison the guards are not allowed to wear guns but this counts as outside. And like so many of his colleagues, he had seen too many movies.

'Turn around then, face against the wall.'

I don't know what he thought I was going to do, because I had already been frisked several times and, even though I am six foot two, he was bigger and had a gun. We were taken across the street and into the court, where the magistrate was another woman, Sharon Grubin. I believe that in a few years the American law-enforcement industry will be dominated entirely by women; probably something to do with all those TV series about female cops, like *Cagney and Lacey*. For six and a half months, almost the only women I saw were doing their utmost to have me put away for years. It was enough to put me off their sex for life, although I was glad to discover later that it had not.

The charge against us – which was to be altered numerous times during the months of hearings – was that we had conspired to sell weapons worth more than $2 billion to Iran, including fighter planes, missiles and tanks. This was said to be a violation of the Munitions Control Act, which prohibits the sale of listed strategic items, made or located in the United States, to countries not approved by the US government. We were also accused of mail and telephone fraud and with conspiring to provide false end-user certificates. (The final version of the charge, in so far as it refers to me, is printed as an appendix on page 191.) The magistrate ordered us to be kept in prison without bail until a further hearing in three days' time, on Friday, 25 April.

Then we went back to the prison and were taken to the

ninth floor, my new home. It is one of the two floors in the MCC reserved for 'prestige' prisoners, arrested for white-collar crimes like racketeering, financial swindles, drug peddling – and arms dealing. In a way it was like checking into a hotel, except that I don't know of any hotels where they make you give up your clothes as you arrive and change into a drab orange uniform, or where they take you into a room and lecture you on what you are and are not allowed to do, or where you are under constant surveillance from guards who watch your every movement on TV monitors.

Each floor has cells on two levels, accommodating around 100 prisoners. My cell was downstairs on B tier, number 913 – unlucky for some. We were two to a cell and I had a number of room-mates. To begin with I shared with a Mafia don, then with Kopka, then Hans Bihn (another fellow defendant) and after that an American who had worked for a well-known pop singer and was there on a drugs charge – like 95 per cent of the people on that floor.

The guards' offices are in a central area, where there is a ping-pong table, a gym, a television and some tables and chairs. A guard usually sits near a pool table in the centre of the space, with three telephones nearby. The main door to the floor is about nine feet wide, made of steel. Normal access is by lift. Prisoners are not allowed into the lift without a guard, in case they take it to the ground floor and make themselves scarce. This means that if you are going anywhere you often have to wait a long time for the lift, until a guard is free.

We scarcely had time to settle in before a fifth member of the group turned up. Hans Bihn was another German who had connections with Minardos (both used to be small-scale shipowners) and who had recruited Kopka and Flearmoy to the enterprise. He had arrived that same morning from Athens and told us ruefully that he had only caught the plane by the skin of his teeth: how he wished he had got to the airport a few minutes later. Hashemi had driven out to Kennedy airport to meet him and they talked in the car before Hashemi was dropped off at the Beekman Tower. Bihn was told he had been booked in at the Vista but, like the other three, ended up in the Customs House car park. They made a video of the arrest and I have watched it: I have never seen a man look quite so be wildered.

Next morning there was a report of our arrest, and a picture, in the *New York Times*. There were two points in it of particular interest. It revealed that at the same time as we were being held in New York, Sam Evans and four of his Israeli contacts had been placed under arrest in Bermuda. Although American law has no standing there, the US customs had persuaded the island's authorities that the five men were going there to perform an illegal transaction and should not be admitted. Bermuda officials refused them entry and tried to put them back on the plane – whose next stop, as luck would have it, was Baltimore, Maryland. When they refused to get aboard they were arrested for violating immigration laws and proceedings began for their deportation.

The second interesting aspect of the report was that the District Attorney for New York, Rudolph Giuliani, had held a triumphant press conference to announce the arrests. One of the problems with the case that became clear to me as it dragged on was that Giuliani is an ambitious politician, by no means the first to use the DA's office as a possible stepping-stone to higher things. The sting may not have been his idea originally, but he seized on it with enthusiasm because to crusade against arms traffickers was a way for him to gain attention and popularity. He fought the case tenaciously even after the Irangate revelations made it hard for all of us to understand why he carried on.

Another official at that day's press conference was William von Raab, the Commissioner of Customs. He used the occasion to describe the defendants in a phrase that stuck with us throughout the months of the proceedings. He said:

You've probably heard of the merchants of death. Well, these people are the brokers of death. They would have operated a terrorist flea market selling everything from conventional weapons to some of the most sophisticated weapons in the world. The Iranians would have used these weapons to make war against their neighbours or to spread international terror against the free west. Without a doubt, the bloody hands of international terrorists would have been on the trigger of the TOW missiles, really an ideal weapon for this dirty business.

I scarcely recognised myself in that description. Hermann Moll, advertising salesman, purveyor of boots, ration packs and other supplies to the armies of the free world – had I now become a 'broker of death'? I suppose it is a matter of opinion, but I was sure of one thing: I would not know what a 'terrorist flea market' would look like.

I obviously needed a lawyer, and so did Kopka. (Minardos had his own lawyer in California and Larry Flearmoy did not seem too interested.) I guessed that Mafia people might be able to give good advice on that score, so we asked around but in the end accepted the recommendation of a Greek prisoner. He gave us the name of the firm he used at Mineola, about twenty miles from New York on Long Island. I rang and they said that two of their partners would come and see us. The one who took my case was Charles Theofan, a small, plumpish, energetic young man who seemed affable and competent.

The first thing he did was to apply for bail. That was when I first used the argument in court that I believed the arms sales were authorised by the US government. Lorna Schofield, the prosecutor, said that was 'preposterous' and the magistrate seemed to agree because she refused bail for all of us.

We had to attend four other hearings in the magistrate's court, before the case was turned over to a judge. I found them increasingly frustrating, partly because of the cumbersome procedure involved in transporting us the few yards from the prison to the Federal Court House.

They begin by waking you ninety minutes early, at 5.30 in the morning, no matter what time your hearing is scheduled. They chase you out of bed and you put on your prison jump suit and go for an early breakfast, while the other prisoners are still in their cells. At 6 a.m. a guard comes up in the lift to collect us. He fills the lift to maximum capacity and takes it down to the third floor. When you leave the lift there are lines drawn on the floor showing where you have to walk. They lead you to a room where you take your prison overalls off and put on your civilian clothes, stored in a plastic bag hanging on a hook. Then you put your prison clothes in the bag. To a man, the guards treat you like filth:

'Stay here.'

'Don't move.'

'Shut up.'

– all in that specially vicious tone of voice I noted in the customs agents when they arrested me.

For two and a half months I had to wear the same shirt in court that I had worn on the night of my arrest. The clean shirt I had brought from London was being held by the prosecution as material evidence. I had nobody in America who would visit me and bring a fresh one. I asked Charlie to oblige but he didn't. Finally I managed to persuade the German Consul to send me one.

From the changing room they lead you along a corridor and put you in a holding pen. There are four of the pens on the third floor – one for women and the other three for men. They are about ten feet by fifteen feet with a concrete bench going round the walls, which are painted in an overpowering shade of blue. Each cell has two barred windows with thick square bars about two inches wide. The glass is half-inch unbreakable Plexiglass. There are usually about thirty men penned into that small space, and on exceptional days as many as fifty. With most of us wearing filthy shirts, all for the same reason, the stench is unbelievable.

By the time you reach the pen it is about 6.30. You stay in there until about 8.10 when they open the door, next to a glass cage with the monitors for the video cameras. The guard reads a list of names and when he reaches yours you go out, handcuffed to the prisoner before or after you.

You walk to the first of two thick metal sliding doors. Everyone is crammed into the space between them, including a guard. Then the first door closes and the second one opens, like an air lock. It leads into a passage, then up a few stairs to the covered bridge between the prison and the marshals' building adjacent to the court. In the marshals' building are five or six more holding pens, each with a window looking into an interior guard area. They put you in one of those and there you sit, with maybe twenty others, from about 8.30 to however long it takes for your case to be reached. It could be mid-afternoon before they reach you and the hearing may be over in a few minutes – and you have been up since 5.30 for that.

Conditions in the pen are squalid. Lavatory paper is scattered over the floor. The only lavatory is behind a thin screen, inadequate to stop people from seeing what you are doing. You have to be fearless to sit on it. On the ceiling of the pen are two video cameras, monitored by a guard in a black glass cage.

Having lunch there is the best thing about it. They get sandwiches from outside, which means you don't have to rely on the muck they serve in prison. Here the sandwiches are usually turkey or prawn salad – not much taste in either of them but at least they are made from decent bread. You also get to talk to prisoners from other floors, a welcome break because you quickly get tired of the people you mix with day in and day out.

I got on well with one of the Mafia men, though. He was a hit man for John Gotti, one of the leaders of the New York Mafia whose name was always in the paper and who was on my floor for a while, although he was not too communicative. His hit man was more ready to talk and we had long conversations in the hours we waited to go into court. He had lung cancer, but he enjoyed fantasising with me about what he would do when he got out of prison.

'You poor guy,' I thought. 'You're going to go down for sixteen years at the very minimum.' And then I thought again. 'What happens if I get put away for the same period, or even longer?' It was a chilling and unnerving thought, but one that kept returning to the front of my consciousness during my time there.

When you are finally called you walk out of the bullpen down the corridor to another steel door, unlocked and open. This leads to yet another space between two doors. Beyond the second set of doors there are two marshals who handcuff you again, this time with your hands behind your back. I was hit by a car when I was sixteen and damaged my neck and as a result I have trouble putting my hands behind my back; but they were not interested.

They take you upstairs to the fourth floor and then to the court room. When the hearing is finished you get one minute to talk to your lawyer. Then the handcuffs go on again and they take you the same way back to the marshals' office, then lock you up again in the bullpen until enough men have gathered to make up a group for a return trip. That can be another couple of hours, because they wait until they have nine or ten people.

The way back to the prison is the same but in reverse. When you get there they lock you up in the holding pen again before you can change out of your smelly shirt and back into your overalls. Going back in, you can be delayed for some time for one of two reasons. The first is if there is a 'move' going on. This means that one or more of the special prisoners on the third floor are being moved. These are government informers, who are either giving the prosecution information in exchange for lenient treatment, or are being sent to other floors to listen in to the conversations of fellow prisoners. Naturally the authorities do not want the other prisoners to know who these 'canaries' are, so they are moved in great secrecy. Curtains are drawn and all traffic through the third floor is halted until they are safely out of sight.

The other delay is when you are unlucky enough to get back during the count, in which case you have to wait in the holding pen until they have finished. They do the count twice a day, to see if they have lost anyone. In the afternoons it is at 4 p.m., which means they have to start counting at 3 p.m. The prison officers are not particularly sharp at mental arithmetic and it can take them three or four counts before they get it right.

When the count has worked they come and call your name and open the door and you go back to the place where your clothes are. There you take off your private clothes and put them in the bag. The guard comes in and makes you stand there naked. The first time I had to do this he barked at me:

'Lift your sack.'

'I beg your pardon?' I replied.

'Lift your sack.'

'I don't understand what you mean.'

'Lift your fucking balls.'

He had a look there, and in my armpits. Then another curious command:

'Bend down and crack a smile.'

'Pardon?'

'Crack a smile.'

'What do you mean?'

'Pull your arse apart,' he shouted in exasperation.

He had a look and was satisfied that, whatever he was looking for, it was not there. So he let me put on my orange jump suit again and give my clothes back.

The odd thing is that when you get back to your floor you actually feel relieved. It is sort of like coming home. When you go to the court building there is absolutely nothing to do. You can't even comfort yourself realistically with the knowledge that the judge or magistrate might set you free. Usually you know they are going to do no such thing, although if only to keep yourself sane you let your hopes rise a bit.

Inside your cell, at least you can sit and read, or put your headphones on and listen to some music. There is no rule against reading in the bullpen but with all those people milling around it isn't easy – and anyway you probably wouldn't be allowed to bring the book back in. There is a great strain on your nerves in all that waiting around in the marshals' pen without anything to do. During a long trial, if you are not out on bail, I don't know how you are supposed to keep your senses together and defend yourself.

Apart from my personal plight, I had two main worries; Noi and my business. Noi was living by herself in our house at Mill Hill in north London. I was able to phone her and reverse the charges because I had transferred some money to her from my account. I phoned her several times every week and became unreasonably neurotic when there was no reply. I feared that it meant she was out with someone else and that I might lose her – and now, more than ever before, I realised how desperately I wanted her to stay with me, and eventually to marry me when we could.

I had a more practical worry about the house. Not long before coming to New York I had used it as security in the deal involving the two Buffalo aircraft for Sudan. Now I was locked away there was every chance that the deal would be aborted and I would lose the house on top of everything else.

I had no confidence whatever in my partner John Saunders – an instinct that turned out to be entirely justified. There were several deals on the boil apart from the Buffalos that needed urgent attention if they were not to fall through, especially the one for the Milan missiles that I had been supposed to go to Portugal to finalise on the day after my arrest. I needed access to an office and a proper telephone, but the magistrate would not grant any of us bail, because the prosecutor said there was a danger that we would flee the country. (In my case, I must confess, she was absolutely right.)

Charlie Theofan proposed to the magistrate that Ralph Kopka and I should be allowed out of prison from 11 a.m. to 6 p.m. on two days a week in his custody and on his recognisance, using the phones in his Long Island office. At first Lorna Schofield said the prosecution had no objection, but she was later countermanded by Giuliani or another of her superiors and they would not agree. As a compromise, they offered to let me use a desk in the District Attorney's office. I think they were hoping to listen in on my phone calls and find something incriminating. Obviously they were disappointed because I was allowed the facility only twice before they complained that it was too great an inconvenience for them, and Judge Sand, the federal judge who had by then taken over the case from the magistrate, withdrew the privilege.

Prison routine did not suit me. One of the worst parts of it was the food. If we were not due in court they woke us at about 7 a.m. and we went to get breakfast. All the food was chilled and then heated in microwave ovens: it was not a kitchen so much as a warming-up centre. The staff stood by the entrance and gave us our plates, then we helped ourselves. A typical cooked breakfast would be scrambled egg. This was usually made with egg powder but if they happened to have some fresh eggs they had a habit of grinding up some of the shell with them, no doubt in the belief that it was particularly nourishing. With them we might get mashed potatoes – made of unpeeled potatoes. You can imagine what it looked like.

Sometimes it was bacon – at least that was what they called it. It was actually just a soft lump of fat. With that we might be offered a portion of what the Americans call breakfast sausage, but which looked to me like a slice of someone's ulcer. On top of the 'cooked' food on the plate, they placed a container of milk and a packet of cornflakes. This carefully thought-out system ensured that the milk and cornflakes box was normally covered with mashed potatoes.

My usual strategy was to take the milk and cornflakes off the plate, scrape off the potato, then go to the dustbin and throw the cooked food into it. One morning I was dropping a slice of breakfast sausage into the bin, when a black hand emerged from behind me and grabbed it.

'How can you throw that away?' my fellow prisoner asked indignantly, and he ate it. No accounting for taste.

For the first three months I lived basically on cornflakes and milk and lost about forty pounds in weight. After that experience at the bin I began swapping my meat for cornflakes with black prisoners. But I was still permanently hungry.

I did, though, have one worthwhile experience in the kitchen. I struck up a friendship with a man who worked there; a tough-looking guy with a good physique, two cauliflower ears and a broken nose. I thought he must be a boxer but he turned out, surprisingly, to be a writer who did body-building in his spare time. His name was Richard Stratton and he was friendly with Norman Mailer, who came to visit him. In the sixties and seventies he had run his own magazine, in which he advocated the decriminalisation of soft drugs such as marijuana. He had been arrested on a charge of importing fifty tons of hashish. I used to talk to him about the iniquities of American foreign policy, especially over Iran and Nicaragua.

I had a lot of time to think about those things, even if my thoughts were obviously coloured by my own experience. I concluded that the Reagan administration are like a bunch of animals with no clue what they are doing, like bulls in a china shop. Any government that is pro-American can get away with anything it wants – look at the Philippines and Haiti. They can kill, torture, whatever, so long as they're pro-American. But anyone who is against America is a terrorist. As for the President himself, here is a man who has the most powerful position in the world and he's not a politician even, but a third-grade actor.

I also talked to Richie Stratton about the prison system. I was thinking at one time of writing a book on it called *Modern Slavery*, because that's what it boiled down to. Where else can you get labour for ten cents an hour? That is the rate they pay you if you volunteer to perform tasks round the prison. One slight advantage is that they unlock your cell door early and you get your breakfast first. But I refused to work.

The only job on offer was on the sanitation team. Larry Flearmoy got obsessed by it. He was taking imprisonment worse than any of us: I could see him visibly going to pieces as the days went on and he must have found the cleaning jobs useful as a kind of therapy. He teamed up with a Greek guy doing five years to life for drugs and gambling. The only thing I heard them talk about was how they could get the

floor more shiny. It irritated me enormously. I shouted to
them that they should get their toothbrushes and shine the
floor with them. When Larry asked me why I did not help, I
told him:

'Larry, I am not moving a finger for these bastards. I
stick within the rules but I'm not moving a muscle for them.
If they expect me to clean the place – no chance.' He
couldn't understand it.

Richie Stratton left after a while and the kitchen work was
taken over by the Mafia. They were there to answer charges
in a case known in New York as the Pizza Connection,
accused of selling drugs in pizza parlours. The food did not
get any better when they took over. In fact the only thing
that changed was that you would see these Italians scurrying
to their cells carrying large boxes of it.

To drink, we usually had decaffeinated coffee – we called
it boiled socks. But from time to time, as a treat, we had
chocolate. We wondered why there was never enough to go
round until somebody went in to the cell of one of the Pizza
Connection people and found 300 bags of chocolate there. I
had noticed that the guy was putting on a lot of weight –
something equivalent to the forty pounds that I had shed.

We passed the time by watching TV, playing ping-pong,
cards or Monopoly. To begin with I played a lot of cards and
dominoes with Nicos, but after a time he got on my nerves,
in spite of his ebullience. He always wanted to be the centre
of attention and the action. He would come back after every
meeting or phone call with his lawyer and say, 'Guys –
beautiful news, we'll all be out of here in a few days' time.' It
went on for months and months. Always, in two or three
days we would be out. But there were times, when it was
obvious that his predictions were not going to be fulfilled,
when he would become very depressed. He was stockily built
when he came in and you could almost see him fading away.
He switched from being exuberant to being dejected. They
took his belt away and he lost so much weight that he had to
go to court with his trousers held up with string.

Later I met three well-educated Pakistanis from the top
tier of our floor, in on drugs charges. They played bridge,

and I made up the fourth. I also spent some time with an Austrian named Rabelbaur, well known in central Europe. He was fighting extradition to Austria, where he was wanted on charges of bribery and tax evasion. I did not share a cell with him because he was a passionate non-smoker, but he came to my cell a lot and we sat and talked.

A lot of the drugs suspects had stories of being caught in sting operations, just as I was. One said he had befriended an American in Pakistan who came back to America with him, saying he could find him a job, then planted cocaine on him just before they landed. Another told me he was trapped by a woman he was living with who turned out to work for the US Drug Enforcement Agency. Some weird people came and went. One man had got $3 million from a bank by computer fraud. They did not know about it until he gave it back, and he was arrested. At one time we had about sixty members of a Chinese extortion gang. One day a Nigerian ship's crew turned up – drugs again. There were a lot of Nigerians and Colombians on drugs charges. One man was deformed because a condom full of cocaine burst in his bowels. They did an emergency operation and he had horrible scars.

For exercise we worked out in the gym or were allowed to go up on the roof for an hour. I enjoyed that, getting fresh air (if that is the word to describe the air in Lower Manhattan) and doing exercises to keep me in some kind of shape. The evenings were broken up by our being locked in our cells for half an hour from nine o'clock. Then we were allowed to circulate for ninety minutes before being locked up for the night at 11 p.m.

It was a prison for men not yet tried or convicted and awaiting transfer to other prisons. The guards called it the Warehouse. My strategy was just to try to get along without any trouble. I had too much to lose to risk being kept there longer than I had to.

I spent a lot of time reading. I got Charlie to bring me in some books about tropical fish and aquaria, my principal hobby. One of the other books I picked up was about the Abscam case, a famous government sting operation similar in some ways to the one I was caught in. In that case, though, the people trapped were officials who had a history of accepting bribes in the past. I know of no other country that allows its law officers actually to trap people into committing offences. They spend thousands, perhaps millions of dollars creating crimes and conspiracies that otherwise would never have happened. The main reason is to make the District Attorney look good and help his political career, no matter who suffers for it. America is a peculiar and pitiless place.

After a month I began to get very miserable. I tried to work out my depression by keeping a diary. I wrote exactly what I felt. If the guards had found it they would have confiscated it, but they did not and I still have it, written in ball-point pen (Charlie used to bring them in for me) on ruled notepaper. In a way it is embarrassing to read it today, when I have been out of prison for many months, but it does show how small things can seem disproportionately significant when you are locked up and bored. Your nerves seem raw all the time, your emotions more intense than when you are leading a full and busy life, with nobody keeping watch over you for twenty-four hours a day. The tone is shrill and bitter and I complain a lot about my conditions. But then, I had plenty to complain about.

The diary begins on Wednesday, 21 May. I record reading in the paper about a former US ambassador to the Vatican, a personal friend of President Reagan, who was discovered selling arms to Libya. But being well connected *he* was not put on trial: he just took early retirement.

'Typical,' I wrote. 'I feel more hate and anger.' And later on I added: 'It is a risk making these notes – Big Brother would not like it – but I have to take it because I want people to know what is happening in this country, to help prevent the same happening in Europe. A world like this is not worth living in.'

I was due in court again the following day and wrote: 'I hope tomorrow for a clean shirt [I did not get it], I hope my lawyer will bring my watch [taken from me when I was arrested] and I hope the judge has informed himself about our case. Last time he knew nothing, not even that there are still people in Bermuda. Will they be extradited?'

The hearing on 22 May was typical of the many I had to endure during the seven months. Court number one in the federal court house is a large, imposing room, probably designed to intimidate both prisoners and spectators by representing the majesty of the law. Its dimensions are some eighty feet by fifty feet, with a ceiling thirty feet high, decorated with a rectangular motif. It was built in the 1930s but in a mock-classical style, its walls covered with wood panelling and black marble and with four large lights hanging from the ceiling. The seal of the United States is on the wall behind the long table, some twelve feet above the floor, where the judge sits, looking lost against such a large-scale backdrop. On his left is a flagpole topped by an eagle, flying the stars and stripes.

Judge Sand was in his sixties, slim and, even in winter, dressed in a light suit that looked as if he'd slept in it. He never seemed to care too much about our case, but I suppose a judge gets that way after a time. Sometimes he would stop the hearing when a lawyer was in the middle of his presentation and once, I am certain, he went to sleep.

The prisoners stand on the left of the judge. In front of the bench is a table used by court officials. The lawyers sit in front of that and the spectators beyond them, separated by a low wooden barrier. Of the four of us in court that day, only Nicos had any relatives to support him – his wife, daughter and two sons had come in from the West Coast. He moved across the room to greet them but was prevented from getting too close by court officers.

The hearing that day was to discuss a date for the full trial. Lorna Schofield said that the prosecution had 200 tapes to transcribe and needed time. They were talking about the autumn. Our lawyers said that was too long and pressed for a date at the beginning of August. Even that seemed an incredibly long time. Ten more weeks – and, already, the month I had spent there so far seemed more like a year.

Judge Sand reserved his decision, as he did on most aspects of the case. Then Nicos's lawyer made representations about bail. He said his client's family, many of them in court, were prepared to put up all they had as bail for him. The lawyer became very emotional and began weeping. 'Look what's being done to innocent people on behalf of the United States government,' he cried. But the prosecutor pointed out that Nicos was a much travelled man with plenty of resources and there was no certainty he would not flee. The judge seemed uncertain what to do but in the end asked both sides to prepare affidavits, so he would have something on paper. Then he went off to lunch.

Back in the changing room I had another run-in with the guard. I had started to put on my prison clothes before he got there.

'Do you always change without a guard present?' he shouted.

'Of course,' I replied. 'As it happens I do not have guards watching me when I change at home.'

He could see I was getting at him. He knew I thought he was a black bastard. So he ordered me to get undressed again. I did and stood there in my underpants for a minute or two.

'Why don't you get dressed?' he asked.

'Because you haven't told me to.'

It was a silly way for me to behave, a petty gesture of defiance, not the action of a grown man. But that's the way the place gets to you: these little irritations prey on your mind because there is nothing else to think about. The routine gets to dominate your life. I suppose it's what they mean by getting institutionalised, or what the Americans more colourfully call Stir Fever.

Back on my floor I had a visit from Charlie Theofan, who arrived as I was in the middle of getting my hair cut. He said it was too early to tell how the judge would react to the requests for bail, but he was fairly sure that nothing much would happen for the next three weeks. I was horrified. The thought of three weeks more in prison was inordinately depressing. And if the judge ruled against bail, which was very possible, the three weeks would stretch into three months. A lot depended on how quickly the Bermudan court came to a decision on whether to order Sam Evans and the others to be sent to the United States. We scanned the *New York Times* every day for news but there was nothing. The morning papers reached us at about 5.30 in the evening, just six for the 100 prisoners on my floor; so it was a scramble to get one.

I did not think I would be able to stand another three months. I was already missing Noi more than I had thought it possible to miss anyone. And that night, when I tried to phone her, I discovered that the phones were out of order. Did they, I wondered, do it on purpose?

My diary shows that the events of the day had put me in a melodramatic mood:

> They make you feel like a piece of shit so that you are demoralised when you eventually stand trial after months of humiliation. Well, they can try with me, but I'll make sure they will not succeed. My love for Noi and my hatred against this regime will help me to keep my dignity. My pride is too strong. When I did my first parachute jump, sitting in a small aeroplane with no door, I said to myself that I shall not start whining like the others in front of me, but I shall go with dignity. It's the same in here. But in the end I will pay them back for every day they have stolen from my life, for every tear my Noi has cried. I will make these bastards pay. I have time enough to think about the ways.

Time was something I had a surfeit of. I would spend some of it sitting in my cell looking out of the small barred window. I could see people wandering towards Chinatown for a meal – real food and not the slop they served in this place. The worst times were when I saw a plane overhead, heading east. How I longed to be on it, flying home to Noi. I thought more and more of London, of shopping with Noi in the King's Road, of walking through Hyde Park and drinking pints of beer in pubs. We had planned to have my parents over from Germany in June, and take them touring in Scotland. I wondered how they had taken the news, and how they had explained things to their friends when they read about me in the papers.

Next day the phone was fixed and I got through to Noi. She asked me how long it was likely to be before I could return to England.

'Could be three weeks, could be four months,' I told her. I thought that four months would be putting the most pessimistic construction on things. Had I guessed that it would take more than double that time to get out of America, my despair would have been total.

A week later, on 29 May, I came out of my cell after the 9 p.m. lock-up and saw the big doors open to admit some new arrivals on to our floor. One of them was a tall, lean man, understandably more dishevelled than when I had last seen him but still with an unmistakably aristocratic air, even in his orange prison uniform. Sam Evans had lost his fight against deportation from Bermuda and had come to join us, along with the four others arrested with him five weeks earlier.

I walked up to him and said, 'Hi, Sam.' He introduced me to the others. The most self-effacing of his companions, who kept himself to himself for the whole time he was in prison, was Avraham Bar-Am, a retired Israeli general still on the army reserve as an adviser to the Northern Army Command. His presence among those arrested in Bermuda had led the press to speculate that the Israeli government were involved in the deal, but this was denied in Jerusalem and Bar-Am would never say definitely one way or the other, although he did once or twice hint that he would have an embarrassing tale to tell if he chose to.

Two other Israelis were Israel Eisenberg, an insurance salesman, and his son Guri. The other man was William Northrop, an American living in Israel, who claimed to be related to the family that owned the Northrop aircraft company. He had been working with Bar-Am to secure some of the supplies. The first words Northrop said to me were 'Can I have a cigarette?' It was his refrain whenever I met him and I took an instant dislike to him.

Next day was the first time that all the participants in the alleged conspiracy got to meet each other. It was like a big reunion except that most of us had not seen the others before in our lives. Sam was the only one who knew us all, and Nicos, who had brought the Israelis into the deal, knew most. Sam and the Israelis were highly indignant at the way they had been treated in Bermuda. They said they had been locked up for twenty-three hours every day, five to a cell with the bathroom just outside. They said the food was terrible, but later admitted that it was not as bad as in the MCC.

I had a long talk with Sam that day about the case. We sat together for about two hours. From that conversation, from reading the court documents later and from talking to some of the characters involved, I was able to piece together the facts about the Israeli side of the Hashemi deals.

Sam had been working on them, in parallel with the negotiations with me and the other London-based dealers, since he began his close relationship with Hashemi in October 1985 – about the time he first approached me. The Eisenbergs had been his first contacts in Israel. He had been introduced to them by Nicos. The Eisenbergs had a company called Bazelet International Trading. When Sam put them in touch with Hashemi, they told him they could supply American-made fighters and transport planes, tanks and missiles worth some $400 million, plus end-user certificates if necessary. Sam confessed that he had always entertained a nagging doubt whether they really had access to such large quantities. He was certain that, if they did, it would not be possible to export them from Israel without American knowledge or approval, so the question of end-user certificates did not really apply. He suspected that the Eisenbergs had simply extracted the details of the weapons from the Israeli air force's catalogue of its surplus arms.

Hashemi was not able to give the Israeli group any better proof of funds than he had given me, and they were as dissatisfied as I was, although Sam did not seem to have any personal doubts that the money was there in Chemical

Bank. In January Sam and Nicos went to New York to discuss the deal with Hashemi, who introduced them to a man he said was a member of the Iranian mission to the United Nations and a co-signatory of the Chemical account. In fact he was a strange figure named Houshang Lavi, a former supplier of American arms to the Shah of Iran who had been working since 1978 as an agent for US government agencies, including the CIA and the customs.

Lavi had been brought in by Joe King, Doyle's superior and the customs investigator in ultimate charge of the case. His role was to persuade Sam and Nicos that they had to telephone the Eisenbergs and Northrop in Israel and make firm arrangements for the delivery of part of the arms package they were offering, with EUCs. That would provide incontrovertible evidence of a conspiracy. The call was made and tape-recorded and Lavi left. As he did so, Joe King went up and embraced him. 'We've got them,' he said. The dealers were not arrested there and then because King wanted to bait the trap for as many as possible, which meant swooping on all of us at the same time. That was Lavi's only involvement in the case prior to the arrests, although he was to surface again later in a significant role.

Sam and Nicos went to Israel in March, and received the impression that their visit was approved by officials. Sam told Hashemi as much in one of their monitored telephone conversations a few days later. Certainly the visitors were able to jump the queue at the airport immigration desk. The Eisenbergs convinced them that at least some of the arms they were offering could be obtained through a company that regularly sold off surpluses for the Israeli Defence Ministry. Sam and Nicos were convinced firstly that the Israeli government approved of the transaction and secondly that this must mean it also had official approval from Washington. That was what Nicos meant when, in conversation with Hashemi, he had spoken about the Israelis not doing it without checking with Momma.

The introduction of Bar-Am into the proceedings in April seemed further proof that the deal was being backed at a high level. Bar-Am said he could provide Russian tanks captured from the Syrians – but these would not have fulfilled Hashemi's condition about their being of US origin. The group met Hashemi in Paris in mid-April, and the Iranian had again brought with him Joe King, whom he described as his associate Joe Jackson. Hashemi took the four men (Israel Eisenberg was not there) to Paris in a private jet. He had arranged for them to be met at the airport by a hired Rolls-Royce and driven to the luxurious Plaza-Athenée hotel, where Hashemi had rented a suite to conduct their business in.

At that meeting four contracts were drawn up for phenomenal quantities of arms: 3750 TOW missiles for $61,875,000; eighteen F–4 fighters for $360 million; a package of Hercules transports, bombs and missiles for $415,130,880; and another 5000 TOW missiles plus miscellaneous aircraft and parts for $343 million. This last contract mentioned the provision of end-user certificates. The seller was a Liechtenstein-based company named Dergo, with which Northrop and Bar-Am were connected.

Hashemi asked them all to go to New York to sign the papers the following week but Evans said that on his trip to Israel he had been told by Israeli intelligence officers not to go to New York 'for security reasons'. Northrop endorsed that warning and King (alias Jackson) suggested that the meeting should take place outside US jurisdiction in the British colony of Bermuda. Hashemi said it should be held on 22 April and promised the Israelis they would be home in time for Passover, four days later. Veillot and de la Rocque were also supposed to be there but by chance, instinct or prior knowledge, they did not turn up. I think it was by prior knowledge, because I believe they were fully briefed about the North transactions. Both men, who travelled on US diplomatic passports, have since gone to ground.

The customs service had warned the Bermuda authorities that the men were going there for a meeting that contravened US law. Special Agent Dennis Fagan wrote to the Bermuda Attorney-General stating:

All of these individuals are traveling to Bermuda for

the sole purpose of consummating a scheme to defraud the United States Government. This fraud concerns the sale of fraudulent documents which would be submitted to the United States Government. These individuals have used a variety of methods to facilitate this scheme, including, but not limited to, fraud by wire and fraud by mailings. This fraud would seek to divert weapons and explosives to certain terrorist groups.

On the basis of this letter the Bermuda immigration authorities refused permission for the five men to enter the country and ordered that they should be put back on to the plane from London, which was flying on to Baltimore. When they refused to reboard, they were arrested and charged with illegal entry. Despite the claim of Evans' lawyers that there was no evidence to support the central affirmation that the group were planning to supply weapons to terrorists, they were deported to the United States five weeks later.

On the day of his arrest in Bermuda, General Bar-Am gave an interview to an Israeli newspaper *Davar*. He said, 'I didn't act in a purely private capacity. Many people in the military establishment knew about the group of which I was an adviser. If the government doesn't intercede on my behalf, if I'm extradited to the United States, I'll make embarrassing disclosures. I'm only a cog in the works.'

He also told the press that after his arrest he called the Israeli military attaché and was told: 'Buddy, you better get yourself the best legal advice available.'

One result of the arrival of the Bermuda group was that progress at last began to be made on the matter of our bail. On the day after they arrived they attended a hearing at which the magistrate set bail of $750,000 for General Bar-Am, although it took him some time to raise the money.

The next day the new arrivals were moved away from our floor to the seventh. I was not sorry to see them go. I did not want to get too involved with them because Charlie thought it would be in my interest to have my case severed from theirs. The transcripts of their taped telephone conversations suggested that they may actually have done some work on getting false EUCs, whereas I had not. So the case against them might be stronger and I did not want to be caught in the fall-out.

There was another reason why I was glad to see them go. I was already getting thoroughly fed up with Northrop. He was a real pain in the neck, always feeling sorry for himself and always scrounging cigarettes. Every single time he met me he asked me for one. I never saw him buy any of his own. He was also a compulsive talker about his case. In prison that can be very dangerous. You have to be careful who you talk to. There are men assigned to reporting what other prisoners say to them: they are known as professional rats. Somebody will share a cell just to get information, and the next thing you know they are in court giving evidence against you on the witness stand. Northrop would run around talking about his case to everybody.

My respite from him was short-lived. After a fortnight he was split from the rest of the Bermuda group and sent back up to the ninth floor with us. Later on the Israelis came back to our floor. Bar-Am was a big, quiet guy – very tanned and always very quiet. He didn't talk much about the case, although he obviously knew more about arms shipments to Iran than anyone else. The Eisenbergs were funny, typically Jewish – the father had been a rabbi. They were supposed to do the insurance for the deal, although I don't suppose that falling victim to a government sting was one of the risks covered.

Hans Bihn originally agreed to co-operate with the prosecution and was on a different floor from us for up to four months after the arrest. He was not named on the first indictment. He told them a lot, until they realised that what he was saying supported the case of the defence rather than the prosecution. So they added his name to the charge sheet later.

Sam's bail was set at $4½ million – a colossal sum but he comes from a wealthy family and raised it within a month. He was released at the end of June. The Eisenbergs went soon afterwards, then Bar-Am managed to raise the money, then Ralph Kopka. They originally asked $2½ million bail for Nicos but his lawyer had it reduced to $800,000 because, alone among the defendants, he is an American citizen resident in the United States and they were able to prevent his departure by confiscating his passport. When I last heard, he was still having to report to the authorities twice a week and was not feeling happy about it.

So it was a depleted group of us who heard the startling news in mid-July that Cyrus Hashemi had died in London. It was an extraordinary, nearly incredible story. He was forty-seven years old and had been perfectly fit, even playing energetic games of tennis, until two weeks before his death. According to his brother he had a full medical examination, including a blood test, in Switzerland three months earlier and was given a clean bill of health. Yet he collapsed in his London office and was admitted to the Cromwell, an expensive private hospital in Cromwell Road, Kensington, where he was diagnosed as having advanced leukaemia. According to the death certificate it was 'acute myeloblastic leukaemia'. The certificate was signed by the deputy coroner for inner west London 'after post-mortem without inquest'.

Just after he died, his brother Mohammed Ali Hashemi (usually known as Jamshid and also then under indictment in America for arms smuggling) told the *Observer* that he believed 'the doctor' had been murdered. He vowed to bring the killers to justice 'even if it takes the rest of my life'. Jamshid explained: 'My brother trod on too many toes. I passed on to him a warning from the Middle East that he would one day have to pay for what he had done, but he laughed it off.'

When Hashemi collapsed, a week before his death, during a meeting with an American businessman, a heart attack was suspected. At the hospital they found his heart sound but performed bone marrow tests and diagnosed leukaemia. That was on 19 July. Treatment was begun the same day but two days later he died. Jamshid said he believed his brother was somehow administered a lethal poison that duplicates leukaemia symptoms. 'Certain Middle East intelligence services are known to use this method,' he asserted. A spokesman for the US customs service in New York told the press that they had been concerned to learn of Hashemi's death and were continuing to investigate it, although no results of any investigation have been disclosed. Scotland Yard say they are not looking into the matter.

According to medical reference books, acute forms of leukaemia can become apparent very rapidly, but it is rare for death to occur so soon. Paul Levitt and Elissa Guralnick's *The Cancer Reference Book* says that, without treatment, the patient with acute leukaemia may die 'within a few months'. It adds that death is usually not from the disease itself but from side effects such as internal bleeding or an infection.

The post-mortem was carried out at Westminster public mortuary by Dr Iain Eric West, head of the Department of Forensic Medicine at Guy's Hospital in London. He could find no other cause of death except leukaemia and added: 'I have found no evidence, from either literature studies or from discussions with colleagues, to suggest that the induction of acute leukaemia would be a feasible method of homicide.'

But the most interesting detail in the post-mortem report was the list of people who were present when it was carried out. There were three: two British policemen and Special Agent McShane, of the US customs. By that time the sting was over. Why were the customs people so interested in how Hashemi died?

At first those of us on the ninth floor were overjoyed at the news of Hashemi's death. This was not primarily because of vindictiveness against the man who had trapped us – although we would scarcely have been human if that had not played a part in it. But we were convinced that without Hashemi's crucial evidence the government would be forced to drop the charges against us. Charlie soon scotched that idea.

'You don't understand,' he told me. 'Hashemi's death is the worst thing possible for you. You won't have him at the trial to cross-examine. All we have now are the tapes of his conversations with you and the others. If he was in court the jury would be able to make a judgement as to whether he was telling the truth, and my guess is that he would have come off badly.'

One immediate adverse result was that the prosecution withdrew an offer to give the defence access to the records of Hashemi's dealings with the government over his own prosecution a couple of years earlier. They used the argument that since Hashemi was dead and could not be summoned as a witness, his character and credibility would not be an issue.

We were convinced Hashemi had been killed, probably poisoned, and one of the defence lawyers called for a new autopsy. He was told that the body had been cremated, so no autopsy was possible. I pointed out to Charlie that Moslems are never cremated, so he made further inquiries and learned that the cremation story was false, but that nobody knew where the body was. Some time later it was discovered that it had been shipped from England and buried quietly in New Jersey. The prosecution had been deliberately lying to try to put us off the scent.

Nor were they helpful when Charlie and the other lawyers asked to review the original autopsy and toxology reports. The prosecution stalled and did not hand them over until April 1987 – after I was back in England. Even then they would only give them to the judge, with a letter from the Cromwell Hospital asking that they not be shown to any of the defendants but that the judge should read out a summary of them.

One of the defence lawyers wanted to ask Dr Elliott Gross, the former Chief Medical Examiner for New York City, to go to England, meet the people who had conducted the autopsy and look at the tissue samples. The prosecution were opposed to it. Lorna Schofield said, 'Let's put the matter of Hashemi's death behind us.'

The judge agreed with her at first. 'Exhuming him is not going to bring him back for the jury,' he stated. Then one of the defence lawyers stood up and said that he had heard from confidential sources that a week or two earlier the US customs had themselves launched their own investigation into the circumstances of the death. The prosecutor said it was the first she had heard of it but, after consulting one of the customs representatives in court, she conceded that it was true. It was clear that a lot was going on without the District Attorney's office knowing.

It remains an unsolved mystery. Charlie had heard before Hashemi died that he had been involved in a dispute with the DA's office, complaining that they had not kept to their side of the bargain because they had not dismissed all outstanding charges against him. Charlie said that, as a result of the row, Hashemi's lawyer had approached the defence team and offered to co-operate with the case; but he had been warned against it by the government.

Potentially the most interesting evidence has come from Houshang Lavi, the US agent who played a walk-on role in Hashemi's negotiations with Sam Evans and the Israeli group in New York in January 1986. He says that at the end of July of that year he was working for the US customs on a case in which they successfully prevented the sale of a quantity of uranium to Libya. He went to see Joe King in his New York office.

'You know the doctor is dead,' he told him.

'Who?' asked Lavi. 'What doctor?'

'Doctor Cyrus Hashemi. You remember that operation you helped us with? Well, we had to get rid of him. He knew too much.'

Lavi did not tape the conversation but he does claim to have a recording of a later talk on the telephone with King, where he, Lavi, raised the question and reminded King about what he had said about Hashemi's death. He says that King did not confirm or deny having said it, but kept silent.

He also recalls that in March 1986, the month before my arrest, he telephoned Hashemi in London from America, to discuss a matter connected with Iran. Hashemi was not there but Lavi left his number for a return call. A few hours later King telephoned him.

'Are you mad, telephoning Hashemi?' he said. 'Scotland Yard is monitoring all his calls. Every time he sneezes there's someone there to hold a handkerchief in front of his nose.'

Lavi is a flamboyant character whose judgement is not necessarily reliable. He claims that he was himself the victim of an assassination plot, involving poisoning his food on a visit to Brussels, and he believes the customs service were behind it. Whether that can be believed or not, there is no reason to question his recollection of his conversations with Joe King. But with my past experience of the system, I am sure that the authorities will do all they can to make sure that the truth never comes out. My belief is that Hashemi *was* involved with Oliver North's White House deals, at least in their early stages, but that everyone is doing their utmost to stop that from being proved. If that is so, it provides a straightforward motive for killing the devious Iranian banker who had so many enemies: me among them. May he not rest in peace.

6

The Long Walk Home

Despite Charlie's warning, echoed in more or less the same terms by the other defence lawyers, we still persuaded ourselves that there was a chance, however slight, that Hashemi's death would result in the case being dismissed. How could they still use the tapes as evidence if the key voice in them was not on hand to be questioned? Charlie said there were ways for the prosecution to get round that, but after three months inside we clutched at any slight hope there was. You begin by expecting at every court hearing that there will be some dramatic new development resulting in your instant release. After a time you realise that it will not happen, that the hearings more often make things worse than better. Hashemi's death was at least something concrete to pin our hopes on, if only for a day or two.

Soon it became clear that the judge would not immediately relent, not even to the extent of granting bail for those of us that the prosecution maintained were too risky to be set free. August came – just as hot and sticky as it is always said to be in New York. The prison was supposed to be air-conditioned, but it never seemed to work properly in the very hot weather. Why bother to fix it for criminals? Sweating in my cell, I could look out of the window and see girls from the nearby shops and offices strolling around with hardly any clothes on. I felt terrible. How I longed to be able to do something quite normal like going up and flirting with one or two of them. And how I longed even more to be back in London with Noi.

The question of my doing a deal with the prosecution for lenient treatment had been raised at an early stage in the case but was quickly abandoned. I had already learned that the government side are not interested in justice or in uncovering all the facts: they only want to know details that will help them gain a verdict of guilty. In a way it is like my own business, selling. If you are a good salesman you don't tell your customers any bad things about your product, only the good things.

All the prosecution want is a conviction. If they get it they are happy and congratulate themselves, regardless of whether the person is truly guilty or not. I could easily have bargained if I had been prepared to invent evidence against some of the other defendants. Lorna Schofield would have been interested in that because it would have helped her case: but she was not interested in what I was prepared to say because I maintained that we were not guilty as charged. That was why she ended the co-operation deal with Hans Bihn: what he told her was the complete truth, and it exonerated us.

Because none of the defendants was prepared to do a deal, the prosecution could not move to a trial confident that they would win the case. As delay followed delay, the defence lawyers were able ultimately to convince even the stubborn Judge Sand that it was unfair to keep us on remand indefinitely. He was at last prepared to concede the principle that all the prisoners should be released on bail. But when it came to setting a sum he dithered again, telling Charlie: 'Make me an offer. Put a package together and put it before me.'

Charlie explained to the judge that I had no funds at all except what I could borrow from my parents and what Noi could get her hands on in London. The court insisted that the person putting up security must be a relative, or someone I would be reluctant to place at a financial disadvantage. (Nicos had got some friends to put up nearly $1 million for him but the judge would not accept it because they were not related to him, so he had to find fresh guarantors.)

At this point something very odd happened. My parents wrote to me from Germany and told me that a man had phoned them and said he was a friend of mine named Bob. He said he had not heard from me for some time and that I seemed to have disappeared. Did my parents know where I was?

They told him about my predicament and he said, 'That's terrible. I'll round up some other friends and we'll put up the bail for him. How do I get in touch?'

They gave him the phone number of the German consulate in New York. He duly phoned there and asked about bail. They said a sum had not yet been agreed and Bob said he would phone the following week to see if there had been any developments.

But he never did make contact again. And the odd thing is that I do not have, and never have had, any friends called Bob. Who was trying to play games with me? And why?

In the end Charlie managed to get the judge to accept a cash payment from me of only $2500, plus a bail bond of $25,000 and another of the same amount from my parents, who had to sign an affidavit to the effect that this was the bulk of their life savings, put by for their old age. It was ludicrous: one day, according to the prosecution, I was a dangerous criminal who could not be allowed out on bail at all. A few weeks later I was worth only $2500 in cash.

I was not going to get my passport back so I could not go home, but at least I would be free to move around the city. By the German constitution no German consulate can refuse to issue a passport to one of their citizens, but, as a condition of my bail, consulates in the United States and Canada were made to undertake to inform the court if I applied for one – which would have meant my immediate rearrest. I was still, therefore, a prisoner in a real sense; but my cage was being made substantially more spacious.

Before my release, though, they had a few more mental tortures and indignities in store for me. The bail figure had been arranged and I was all set to leave the MCC after six and a half months. My possessions, such as they were, had been packed away in a box for me to take. You can imagine the feeling. At last I was getting out. Hans Bihn and an Austrian acquaintance we made in prison had both been out for a few weeks, and we planned a monster celebration in an Austrian bar downtown that they had discovered.

The long rigmarole about getting from the jail to the court seemed less oppressive that day. In court the bail conditions were spelled out. The judge was happy and I thought my release was certain. As a formality, the prosecution were asked if they agreed. Lorna Schofield rose and said:

'Your honour, we agree, but . . .'

My heart sank. 'But' can be the cruellest word in the English language.

'. . . but the affidavit from Moll's parents is incomplete. It doesn't say that they understand that if Moll does not comply with the bail conditions, their money will be forfeit.'

I was furious. Everybody knows what a bail bond is. The whole point of it is to provide security against someone not showing up for his trial. But the judge, on this occasion, did not hesitate.

'Get a new affidavit,' he sighed.

So instead of going out on the town with Hans and the Austrian, I found myself back in prison making furious phone calls to the German consulate asking whether they could get a new affidavit sent over from Germany in the next twenty-four hours, or at least a telexed confirmation that it was being sent. Only Larry Flearmoy and I were still left inside. It was a depressing day. In my cell on my own, I scarcely slept at all.

The German consulate staff are efficient, I will give them that. Next morning the Consul turned up at the court house with a telex confirming that the new affidavit had been lodged with the German Foreign Office in Bonn. At about 10.30 in the morning a guard shouted:

'Moll, get your things, you're going out on bail.'

I never thought I would actually get pleasure from anything said to me by one of my tormentors. I went through the routine of going to the court house for what I was determined would be the last time. Collecting my box of possessions again I went to the office to get a pass. Then there was the standard half-hour wait for the lift. As I was waiting one of the senior guards came up and said:

'Where are you going with that stuff?'

'Out on bail,' I replied triumphantly.

'Ah, we'll see you again,' he grunted, and I thought, 'Not if I have anything to do with it.'

In the changing room on the third floor I put on my civilian clothes, handed back my blanket and left my box of things to be collected later. But I was still in handcuffs and was put in the familiar holding pen for nearly an hour, before being taken to the marshals' holding pen for the best part of three hours.

Finally I went through another double door to where two plain-clothes marshals were waiting to take me through the court building to the room where I had to sign my bail bond. An official read out the terms of bail; things I could and could not do. When he had finished he asked:

'Do you agree?'

'Yes.' I would have agreed to anything.

'Sign there.'

When I got downstairs I was met by the German Consul, Ulf Hanel, who had been waiting nearly four hours. But still the bureaucracy was not over. The handcuffs went on again as I was led back to the marshals' office, then they were removed while I sat outside a room containing a computer terminal. It is where they run your name through to see if there are other charges against you anywhere else in America. If so, you go inside again. I heard of one man who had to go back because he had an alimony payment outstanding.

When my name provoked no spark of recognition on the screen, Hanel said, 'Let's get out of here.'

'I couldn't agree more,' I replied fervently.

The feeling of just walking through the court building without handcuffs, for the first time in six and a half months, was tremendous. Just getting into a lift, without waiting for a guard, seemed like bliss. Then, at last, I was outside on the street. Although it was October the weather was still warm and people were taking the chance of wearing their summer clothes for the last time before putting them away until next year. The city's mood seemed relaxed. It was like breaking out of a cocoon and starting a new life.

'Let's go and get some lunch,' said Hanel. 'Do you like Chinese food?'

Anything that was not the bland, nondescript stodge of the prison would have been welcome. There was, too, a certain pleasure at the prospect of being able to walk freely round Chinatown, where I had been gazing out of my barred window for so long.

We went to a restaurant Hanel knew, on the first floor of a cramped building in one of the narrow side streets of the district.

'I know what your first order will be,' he said, and immediately called up four beers – three for me and one for him. He had obviously done this kind of thing before. I chose Chinese rather than American beer, because I was not feeling especially affectionate towards anything American. The meal was a revelation, cooked with skill and care, using herbs and spices to make it taste good, rather than slung together and warmed up just to fill a man's belly with the regulation quantity of stodge.

Afterwards Hanel had to hurry back to the consulate. He had given me $900 that had been sent by my parents, so I was not penniless. But there I was, after being locked away for six and a half months, standing in the middle of Chinatown not knowing where to go or what to do.

I had made an arrangement with Hans Bihn that I could stay with him for a while. He was going to lodge with his brother in a rooming house in Westport, Connecticut. I had not the first idea how to get to Westport and I did not have his phone number. His lawyer would know but I did not know *his* number either, so I phoned Charlie, who was supposed to have been at court that day to see to my release. When I got through to him the first thing he said was:

'Hermann, I'm so sorry. I couldn't make it today but I promise you I'll get you out tomorrow.'

'Charlie,' I said quietly. 'I am out.' The trouble with

American lawyers is that they are always too busy to look after all their clients properly.

'Son of a gun,' he shouted. 'Where the hell are you?'

'I'm standing in the middle of Chinatown with nowhere to go. The German Consul got me out. If it had been up to you I'd still be inside.' Charlie let my bitterly felt insult pass.

'Good to hear you're out, anyway.'

He gave me the number of Hans's lawyer and from him I got Hans's number. Hans told me how to get to Westport.

Grand Central Station is not the most suitable place for someone still disoriented from being cooped up for months. It is full of people scurrying around with no time to help you find the right platform. But I saw a train announcement board through the crowd, bought a ticket, found the train and sat on it. All the time, I could not get rid of the fear that any moment someone was going to come up behind me, put a hand on my shoulder and shout:

'Moll, come with me.'

It is a seventy-minute journey from New York to Westport. Hans was waiting for me at the station exit with his brother.

'How are you?' he inquired.

'Thirsty,' I announced decisively.

We walked about half a mile to the downtown area and the nearest bar. Gin-and-tonic time at last. Hans and his brother obviously had no money, so the drinks were on me. They were in any case drinking beer and cheap wine. We stayed until midnight and my bill came to $55 – about $40 of it for my gins. Although I had eaten nothing since lunch, I still could not get myself drunk. I had thought that after six and a half months I would be totally insensible after a couple of beers; but no matter how much I drank I stayed sober.

We took a taxi to the house, which was about five miles from the centre of Westport. It was a large, wood-framed house, characteristically American; but as soon as I stepped inside I recognised that it was completely disorganised, dirty and an utter shambles. Hans's brother had found it when he came to Westport to pursue an affair with a married woman he had met in Germany. The landlord's wife came from Cologne. The first night I shared Hans's room. Before we went to sleep we polished off a jug of cheap wine between us, but I still did not feel at all tipsy.

Next morning I awoke and wondered whether I had been dreaming it all. But a quick glance round the room confirmed that I was no longer in my prison cell. After a shower I had my first meeting with the landlord. He was a short man and immensely fat, like a globe on two legs. He did not work and spent the whole day, as I was later to discover, sitting around the house and talking about money.

We agreed a rent of $400 a month, which seemed steep but I wanted to be with Hans because I had no other friends in the New York area. I paid a month's rent in advance. Then I walked into Westport with Hans to buy some clothes. There was no other way of getting to the town except by taxi, and we certainly could not afford that every day. In any case I was still feeling the need to get out and take exercise, as a reaction to being locked up. It was a difficult walk because the Americans, who regard walking as an eccentricity, do not put footpaths alongside their roads. (One night, coming back from an evening's drinking, Hans was knocked into a ditch by a passing car. Luckily he was not hurt badly.)

I went to a men's outfitter and told the salesman that an airline had lost my luggage and I needed a whole set of new clothes. I put them on in the shop and threw my prison underwear and dirty shirt into a rubbish bin. I needed some shoes, too: the expensive crocodile-skin pair I had brought from London were not going to last many five-mile marches in and out of town.

With the shopping over, we went to a bar and spent most of the rest of the day there. That quickly became our regular routine. We would wake up in the morning and ask, 'Where are we going to get drunk today?' It was a demoralising way of life but it was almost impossible to stay in the house even if we had wanted to. The prospect of spending the day with the fat landlord, with his obsession with money, was too depressing to contemplate. We left the house at 8.30 every morning, before he returned from taking his wife to work.

Westport, Connecticut, is a smallish town, planned to

accommodate the motor car and inconvenient for people who do not possess one. It is fairly prosperous with many big wood-framed houses such as the one I was staying in. Apart from the general air of chaos and mess in the house, there were the cats – eight of them – two parrots and a senile dog called Buddy. It was the sort of place where you would go into the kitchen and see the cats nibbling at the family's food. It was strange because the landlady, being a strict Orthodox Jew, made a lot of fuss about the food and implements being Kosher. I am sure that having things licked by cats does not conform with the rules.

One night I came home drunk at 2 a.m. Everything was dark and the front door was locked. I went in the side way, through the garage, unable to see a thing because the light switch was at the far end. I put my right arm in the parrot cage and one of the parrots bit my finger. The cage fell down on to Buddy, who barked, and naturally the parrot was squawking like mad. As I stumbled up the stairs from the garage, I stepped on one of the cats, who gave a loud yelp. By this time everyone in the house had woken up and come out of their rooms in their night clothes to see what had happened. It was like a scene from some crazy farce.

I had to take the train to New York every couple of weeks for court hearings. At the first of them following my release, I was horrified when one of the prosecution lawyers told the judge: 'I have to report that defendant Moll has violated his bail terms.'

That is not at all the kind of thing you like to hear in those circumstances. The prosecutor explained that I had not reported to the Department of Pre-trial Services every few days, as prisoners on bail are supposed to do, to confirm that I had not fled. Charlie explained that, no doubt through an oversight, I had received no instructions about reporting. He added that since I had not in fact tried to flee the country I should not be penalised for a bureaucratic mistake.

Technically the judge could have put me back in prison, but he accepted Charlie's argument. From then on I had to phone the department regularly and go to see my case officer whenever I was in Manhattan for hearings. On these visits I explored the bars near the court house. I felt I needed a drink or two before I went into court, because the judge was always so indecisive that it infuriated me.

The Austrian bar we had been told about proved as good as its reputation. It was Die Fledermaus in Water Street, near the Staten Island Ferry at the bottom end of Manhattan. It was owned by a couple of Austrians who I became quite friendly with. They served German Dinkelacker lager and real German food – sausages with sauerkraut and Wiener schnitzel. We would spend the evenings there after the hearings. It was as near as we could get to forgetting we were in that oppressive city and pretending we were back in Germany.

But there were times, after the prosecution had requested and been granted yet another delay in the proceedings, when there seemed no prospect of our ever being given our passports back so that we could leave. As the days grew shorter and Christmas approached, I began to despair and seriously to work out ways of fleeing the country.

I had two plans. Plan A was to fly down to El Paso in Texas, just across the Rio Grande from Mexico. I would take a bus into Mexico for a day trip and simply disappear. Since the border guards mostly look for illegal immigrants going in the opposite direction – *to* the United States *from* Mexico – I reckoned that my chances of making it were good. I would find my way to Mexico City and get a travel document from the German consulate there, which was not under the same obligation as the consulates in America and Canada to inform the US authorities. Then I would fly back to London. Since my supposed offence was not against the law in England, the Americans would not be able to extradite me and force me to go back.

I had even gone so far as to buy detailed maps of the border area around El Paso. I had read stories of how illegal Mexican immigrants simply swam or in some cases walked across the Rio Grande into the United States, because there was no border fence. I was sure it must be just as simple to do it from north to south.

For Plan B, I had made less detailed preparations. In

outline, it would have involved going to an East Coast harbour in Canada or America and stowing away on a ship, or bribing the captain with a few thousand dollars to take me to Greece or wherever he was going. It was the sort of scheme that works in the movies but I thought that on balance the Texas plan was preferable, because it did not rely on the goodwill or corruptibility of any other party.

I know that both plans sound a bit fantastic, like something out of a boy's adventure book. But what had happened to me so far was not exactly like normal everyday life. I had been living in a fantasy world for more than seven months – not my own fantasy but one imposed on me by the American authorities. I probably would have had a go at the Texas scheme before long, had something not happened to alter my prospects critically.

It is fatal to lose hope. I clung to the knowledge that what I had maintained about secret American approval for arms sales to Iran was right and would one day come out into the open. I knew that the Americans were not good at keeping secrets: it was just a matter of time. But I was in no position to know just how much time it would take, or whether I would be able to wait.

On the morning of 5 November 1986, it happened. It was Hans who gave me the news after he had been alerted by the landlord.

'Seen the paper?' he asked. When I said no he pushed it in front of me.

The main story told how two days earlier a Lebanese magazine, *Al Shiraa*, reported that Robert McFarlane and others had visited Tehran in May to talk to officials about arms supplies and the release of hostages, and that some arms had actually been transported on the plane the delegation had travelled on. At that stage the papers only knew a small part of the story and had not thought of a catchy name for it. And they had yet to make the vital connection with the supply of arms to the Contra rebels.

I got hold of Charlie as soon as I could. During the whole case so far he had made it his business never to be too optimistic about my chances of release, so as not to raise my hopes too high. But even he had to admit that it was hard to see now how the government could go ahead and prosecute the case against us. I decided to shelve my escape plans.

The first response to the reports of the Iran arms deals from Washington officials, on the instructions of Admiral Poindexter, was to say nothing, although Shultz was keen to bring the facts into the open right away. On 4 November Larry Speakes, President Reagan's spokesman, said, 'As long as Iran advocates the use of terrorism, the US arms embargo will continue.' But the same day Hashemi Rafsanjani, the Iranian Speaker, confirmed that the McFarlane visit had happened, while denying that the Iranian government had been involved in planning it – indeed he asserted that McFarlane and his companions had been sent packing soon after their arrival. The day after that, President Reagan said the stories about the visit had 'no foundation' and tried to discourage further speculation by saying it would harm the chances of the remaining hostages being released.

But his denial could not be sustained and the story would not go away. Inevitably the questions from the Washington press corps became more and more persistent. On 9 November, a fresh statement was issued, making it clear that the policy of supplying arms to Iran *had* been approved at a high level inside the administration and that this represented a switch in previously stated policy. Three days later Reagan confirmed this in a meeting with members of Congress, attended by Vice-President George Bush. On the same day Larry Speakes and a spokesman at the Justice Department both stated that Edwin Meese, the government's senior law officer and the man behind the prosecution of the case against me, had known of the arms sales at least since the President's Finding was signed in January 1986, three months before my arrest.

On 13 November the President gave a televised address about the affair, in a vain attempt to prevent it from turning into a major scandal. He said the supplies of arms consisted of 'small amounts of defensive weapons and spare parts', just enough to fill a transport aircraft and not on a large enough scale to influence the outcome of the war with Iraq. He admitted that diplomatic contacts with Iran had been under way for eighteen months, in other words since the summer of 1985. The object, he said, was to obtain the release of American hostages. One shipment of arms had gone to Iran on the very day that one of the hostages, Rev. Benjamin Weir, had been released. But Reagan denied that there had been any straight arms-for-hostages swap.

In a later interview, however, he used the word 'trade' to describe the transaction. Inconsistencies in Reagan's remarks greatly damaged the government's credibility and fuelled the controversy. The following day an Israeli official added a new dimension to the affair by admitting that Israel had been supplying arms to Iran since as long ago as 1982, with explicit American approval.

All this confirmed absolutely the statements I and the other defendants had made all along about covert American policy on arms sales. And later, when new details emerged about the huge quantities involved, our defence seemed to get stronger and stronger. Here at last was the light at the end of the tunnel that I had been awaiting for so long, its beam growing stronger as more details were published in the newspapers. This time, surely, they could not stop me from leaving the country.

In the long term, they could not but, characteristically, they took their time in reaching a decision. On 17 November Judge Sand asked Lorna Schofield whether the Washington revelations had changed the government's view on whether to go ahead with the case. She insisted that the show would go on, maintaining that the charges against us had nothing to do with the Iran arms revelations because our main offence had not been trying to sell arms to Iran but conspiring to defraud the US government with false end-user certificates.

Even Judge Sand recognised that the daily press revelations were altering the position radically. His attitude towards us softened notably, although he was still reluctant to reach any firm, unequivocal conclusion. There were judges, said

Charlie, who would have dismissed the case there and then: not Judge Sand. The following month, a judge in Texas did release a man convicted of selling arms to Iran, on the grounds that the US government had done the same thing. The Irangate story did not die down and the President was forced to hold a press conference on 19 November. Taking full responsibility for the decision to go ahead with the arms sales, he said, 'While the risks were great, so too was the potential reward. Bringing Iran back into the community of responsible nations, ending its participation in political terror, bringing an end to that terrible war, and bringing our hostages home – these are causes that justify taking risks . . . and we're going to continue on this path.'

When he spoke of hostages I wondered whether he had considered the position of myself and the others, held against our will in what to most of us was a foreign and hostile country. And I wondered just how well informed he was when he made this statement about the TOW missiles: 'This is a purely defensive weapon. It is a shoulder-carried weapon and we don't think that in this defensive thing – we didn't add to any offensive power on the part of Iran.' If someone tried to carry a TOW on his shoulder, he would get very sore. He must have been confusing it with a Milan missile, which is shoulder-carried. Some President, who can't even distinguish between American weapons and French.

Reagan was asked several times whether the United States had any role in the supply of arms to Iran by the Israelis before 1986, and each time he denied it. It did not take journalists long to discover that in doing so he was lying – either on purpose or because he had not been properly briefed – and his denial was reversed by officials.

The President had also understated the quantity of the arms sent to Iran. The following day it was revealed that more than 2000 TOW and 235 HAWK missiles had been supplied – more than had by then been admitted but, even so, far fewer than the actual quantity as disclosed later. And a few days after that the diversion of funds to the Contra guerrillas came into the open.

On 25 November Admiral Poindexter resigned as President

Reagan's National Security Adviser, and Colonel Oliver North was dismissed from his post at the National Security Council. Next day, Senator John Tower was appointed to head a three-man team looking into arms supplies to Iran and Nicaragua. Even the prosecution had to admit that the revelations might affect the case against us. Benito Romano, a colleague of Lorna Schofield, told the judge, 'Obviously new facts have come to light that must be fully developed and assessed. . . . we are attempting to review the entire situation in the light of recent disclosures.'

The judge said that I and the other overseas defendants could book seats on planes in the hope that he might be able to let us go home for Christmas. But I could see my money was not going to last even that long, so I racked my brains for ways of earning more. I realised the only thing I had to sell was my story, which, following the Irangate scandal, could be a valuable property.

I phoned the New York offices of German magazines and television stations to offer them interviews. The first was with ZTF, a TV channel, and they paid me $400. The interviewer asked me if I would sue the US government for wrongful imprisonment. I said I would sue them for $20 million, including the $2 million worth of business I had lost as a result of not being in London. I still might do that, depending on how the case turns out. Then I did an interview with *Der Spiegel*, who put me up for a couple of nights in the Inter-Continental Hotel, off Park Avenue, and paid me $700.

I agreed to be interviewed by the American networks, too, but I did not get paid for those. After one of them I went to an Irish bar on the other side of Foley Square that I had come to patronise before and after the hearings. I was in there when one of my interviews came up on the television set behind the bar. The other drinkers recognised me and were impressed.

'Say,' they drawled in some awe, 'so you're one of the brokers of death?' When I confirmed that I was, their reaction was interesting. After all the propaganda and lies the prosecution had spread about me and the other defendants, it would not have surprised me if the people in the bar shunned me. But they were quite willing to listen to my explanation of what happened and when I had finished they expressed their sympathy and support in the most practical way – they stood me drinks for the rest of the evening. I have no quarrel with the American people, just with their government.

One evening, returning by myself from a court hearing and a swing around the Manhattan bars, I had one of those rare lucky breaks that a man in my position needs but which had been notably missing from my life for most of the year. It was pouring with rain when the train arrived at Westport. Walking to the house was out of the question so I jumped into a taxi. Sharing cabs is normal in Westport and I found a woman in it already. She was in her thirties, not beautiful but well groomed and wearing an expensive fur. We had both been drinking a bit so we were quite talkative, and within no time I had discovered that her name was Sally, she had been married and was now divorced. We sparked something in each other: I suppose that, in our different ways, we were both terribly lonely. I asked her out for a drink and we found we got on famously.

She took me to her house quite close to the town centre. It was a remarkable building, a converted church with a large open fireplace, certainly a distinct improvement on the appalling place I was then living in. That first night we talked for a long time before, very late, I went back to my rooming house. But we soon became lovers: I used to stay with her quite often.

She also had an apartment in Manhattan, on West 57th Street in the exclusive Sutton Place district. This was of the utmost convenience, for it meant I had somewhere to stay while the numerous court hearings were in progress as we tried to persuade the judge to let me have my passport back and leave the country at last. She also took me to spots that I would not otherwise have had access to, but which more suited the lifestyle I had left behind in London – places like the Tiger bar at the Princeton Club, where she was a member. This was where the city's real movers and shakers congregated. If only I was free to do business, I might have found some customers there. . . .

Having a Manhattan base also meant that, for the first time, I could wander around New York. I had come to know the area near the court house quite well by now, but the rest of the city I had only glimpsed all too briefly from the top floor of the Beekman Tower on the night I was arrested. When I explored it at ground level it did not take me long to conclude that it was the dirtiest city I had ever seen. I have been to Bombay, Calcutta and Colombo: somehow you accept that these Third World places are going to be squalid and filthy. You don't expect the ultra-modern New York, home of big business and high technology, to be as bad; but it is.

In some parts the smell of sweat can be overpowering. Homeless people sleep in the streets or in the railway and bus stations, ignored by everyone except the police, who from time to time wake them and force them to find a new place to shelter.

I have two abiding memories of Grand Central Station. I saw a man sitting on the station floor picking his toes and felt utterly nauseated. And when I bought a hot dog at the station while waiting for the train, I was amazed to see a black hand suddenly appear over my shoulder, extract the sausage from the bun and make off with it. It reminded me of the man who did the same thing with the breakfast sausage I was throwing away at the prison cafeteria.

Times Square and the streets around it provided the most astounding and most sleazy experience I had in New York. There is no equivalent to it in Britain or in most of Europe. Drugged, listless and sometimes apparently insane men and women hang around on the corners, their eyes unfocused, dealing in drugs quite openly. The pornography shops, with video booths and live strippers, are squalid enough to put you off sex for life – and if they don't the hookers will; the ugliest I have ever seen, hanging around on corners and in hotel doorways looking half dead. You would have to be very desperate to go with one of them. Even if you survived without being robbed, I should think you would catch every disease under the sun.

It is certainly not the exciting downtown area it is made to seem in some movies: at night the main excitement is to get out without losing your wallet. The people there are openly destroying their own lives and other people's, yet the law-enforcement authorities do almost nothing about it. Instead, they devote their resources to attempting to create crimes where none hitherto existed, so as to trap law-abiding business people like me.

Even my experiences of New York's famous and glamorous restaurants were bad. I went to a well-known midtown steak house one lunchtime when I felt like a decent meal and was fed up with Chinese. I was foolish enough to let the waiter recommend the pheasant. It was not properly hung and was consequently very tough, with the texture of a rubber duck. It looked as though it had 10,000 flying hours behind it and on top of all that it was overcooked. In truth it was inedible. I complained to the waiter and the manager but they were abusive and I still had to pay $68 for dinner for one.

I had never been to the United States before and had never really been attracted to it. From the point of view of my business there had never been any need to go there. Most of my deals are done with Middle East countries. Americans are sellers not buyers in the arms market so there are no customers to visit. Nor do you have to cross the Atlantic to buy American products: they are available almost anywhere in the world. So this, my first reluctant visit to the promised land of the west, would, if I had my way, certainly be my last.

Sam, who had been staying with a friend in midtown Manhattan, was the first to get his passport back. All of us were hoping that we would get home for Christmas but, as the prosecution put still more petty obstacles in the way, it became apparent that we would not. One question that delayed proceedings was whether the Israeli defendants would be prevented by their government from going back to New York for the trial. If reports were true that the Israelis were playing a large role in procuring arms for Iran, then the government might well prefer not to have the Eisenbergs, Northrop and particularly Bar-Am subject to vigorous cross-examination in an American court.

There was also a suggestion that the prosecution of our case might be taken over by Lawrence Walsh, the independent counsel appointed by the President to prosecute cases arising out of the Irangate affair. If he had agreed to take over it would have been a boon for the defendants, because it would have amounted to an official admission that our case was connected with the arms deals masterminded by Oliver North.

The prosecution always insisted that there was no connection between the cases. Lorna Schofield said in November that Admiral Poindexter had assured her that the defendants played no role in any official deals. I am certain he was lying. She also maintained, as a clinching argument, that there was one crucial difference: in the North deals, no false end-user certificates had been drawn up. That was a meaningless point because our group had not obtained any false certificates either. We had only talked about it, just to impress the customer.

Until Walsh's decision not to take over the case was known in January, the judge would not let any of us leave the country. But even when it became clear that we were going to be allowed to go home, things still moved agonisingly slowly, and by February I was desperately short of cash. The money from my parents and from the German interviews had long since disappeared, much of it having gone to enrich the bar owners of Westport and Lower Manhattan.

Sally had agreed to lend me the extra $1500 I needed for surety, as the price of getting my passport back, but I thought it prudent not to stay in her apartment for what I thought would be my last few days in America. Instead I stayed at a hotel in Hempstead, near Charlie's office. Like the other defendants awaiting the judge's final clearance, I was in a state of permanent suspension. We were in court nearly every day. It always looked as if we were going to be released in the next day or two, but every day one more snag would crop up.

As well as the $1500, I needed bonds signed by my parents and by Noi for an extra $50,000, beyond the $25,000 my parents had pledged already. The court also wanted confirmation from the German embassy that my parents' bond was legally enforceable. I was still booking flights to London almost every day until, on 17 February, it looked as though I would get away that night. But the hearing was so delayed that there was not time to do all that had to be done before I could leave. My dilemma was that I had by then run out of cash.

On 13 February I had moved into the Gramercy Park Hotel on Manhattan to be close to the court and handy for the airport. But that was $100 a night, so next day I moved into a cheap and none too savoury place in the Times Square area. But after the hearing on the 17th I counted the money in my pocket and it came to eighty cents. I did not even have the fare to take a subway from the court house back to the Times Square hotel. I had always read that New York was the world's worst city to be penniless in, and now I was having first-hand experience.

I did, however, have my Visa credit card. There is one hotel within walking distance of the court house. Ironically, it is the Vista Hotel in the World Trade Center – the hotel that some of my co-defendants thought they were being driven to when they were arrested the previous April. It is right alongside the US customs headquarters, where we were all taken for our initial processing. I did not relish the thought of spending my last night in New York so near a place with such unpleasant memories, and at $240 a night the hotel was absurdly expensive: but I had no choice.

I felt a pang of dread as I passed the Customs House. Was there someone waiting inside to jump out and haul me in and start the whole sequence again? Nothing happened, of course. As a member of the Hilton/Vista club I got a superior room on a high floor and was allowed to keep it until 6 p.m. the following day – surely long enough for the formalities to be completed. And as long as I stayed in the hotel I could charge my whole life to my Visa card – phone calls, meals, drinks, even cigarettes from the news-stand.

I solved the problem of how to get to the airport by booking Upper Class on Virgin Atlantic, which includes free limousine service. I had reason to be thankful for the cashless credit-card society, but reflected how odd it was that when you had no money you were forced to use the most expensive services. In my excitement and anticipation I could scarcely sleep, so I watched two of the movies on the cable TV in my room – another $14 charged to the card.

I was supposed to meet Charlie at the court canteen at eleven next morning for the final formalities. He was two hours late. I sat in the canteen nursing the one cup of coffee I could afford. By the time he turned up I was a nervous wreck. He took me to the bail office where I paid the $1500 Sally had lent me and signed a bond for $80,000: I would have signed for $80 million if they had asked. From there I had to go to the prosecutors' office to hand over some documents and get them to phone the customs people and ask for my passport back.

I could not bear to go into the office where I had first met my tormentor Lorna Schofield, so I made Charlie go in by himself. It took him half an hour. Then we went to the Customs House, where Charlie asked to see Dennis Doyle, the man with the pock-marked face who had been in charge of my arrest. I had insisted on Charlie coming because I had heard that when Ralph Kopka had gone to collect his passport a few days earlier, Doyle had kept him there for an hour in a last desperate effort to force a 'confession' out of him. Even though I had nothing to confess, I did not relish seeing Doyle alone.

It is hard to describe the blissful feeling of having my passport in my pocket again. It is a routine little book that everyone takes for granted – until it is forcibly confiscated from them. Then, you feel like a bird with its wings chopped off: unable to fly and vulnerable to countless predators.

To celebrate I took Charlie out for a late lunch at the Vista. The bill came to $90 but I signed for it cheerfully, reflecting that he had deserved it, despite the constant irritations of trying to track him down, not to mention his habitual lateness. I went back to my room for a bath and to pack the few things I had. Just before six o'clock I paid the bill – $544.27 for twenty-four hours in a hotel, including the movies, meals and dozens of phone calls. The limousine came at seven and drove me to Newark airport for the 10 p.m. takeoff.

I was relieved that they accepted credit cards in the airport bar. After I had checked in for the flight I sat with relays of gin-and-tonics in a state of almost unbearable tension, dreading the prospect of my name being called over the loudspeaker. That would have meant that they had found yet another excuse to stop me leaving and I worked out what I would do if it happened. I would have rushed out, grabbed a taxi to Manhattan, jumped out of it without paying and disappeared in Grand Central Station, where I would have smuggled myself aboard a train to Canada. Every time an airport announcement was made, I started to feel sick.

'Upper Class passengers can board at their convenience,' said the attendant at the departure gate. My convenience was right away, thank you ma'am. I was in my seat almost before she had finished her announcement. On the aircraft I felt a bit more secure. I felt even better when we began gaining speed up the runway and took off. I got a final, hateful view of the lights of Manhattan before we headed east across Long Island to the Atlantic. At last, I was out of their reach.

I was keen to share my relief with the other passengers. The drinks came round and I was not slow to pour out my story to everyone within earshot. When I told them what had happened they sympathised, congratulated me on my eventual release and helped me celebrate with the airline's free champagne. Virgin Atlantic is proud of the reclining seats in its Upper Class section, which allow passengers to stretch out full length to sleep. I am afraid they were wasted on me. Sleep was out of the question.

It was a cold, crisp, mid-February morning. The sun had been up for a couple of hours and was shining on the Sussex countryside when the jumbo jet arrived at Gatwick airport. Everything looked so normal that I wondered fleetingly whether the last ten and a half months had all been a dreadful nightmare that I had dreamed up on the flight home. Then I wondered whether this was all a dream, and I was still dozing fitfully in my room at the Vista.

I had no baggage to wait for and went straight through the green customs channel: nothing to declare except my undying resentment of the United States of America. It was only when I saw Noi waiting beyond the customs hall that I knew this was no dream. It was marvellous to see her again after those long months. She looked thinner than when I left – as indeed I was – and you could tell from her face what a strain my absence had imposed on her.

The airline limousine drove us to the ground-floor flat in Cricklewood that used to be my office. Noi had done as well as she could to make it comfortable, but it still had the air of a hurriedly abandoned place of business. There were bare wires where the telex machines had been ripped out. The file drawers were nearly empty, and it seemed that my ex-partner John Saunders had been through them and removed material relating to ongoing deals. I was subsequently told that some of them were completed, but if that were so I never saw any of the money. I also blamed him for the loss of my house in Mill Hill, which had been used as security in the Buffalo aircraft deal with Sudan. I believe John now lives in Saudi Arabia and I hope for the sake of his health that we do not meet again. For my part I would love to get my hands on him.

The desolation of the Cricklewood flat could not have symbolised more vividly the ruin of my business. To my mind, the American authorities were entirely responsible for it. Everything would have to be built up again, almost from scratch.

But not quite yet. I was in a mood to postpone as long as I could the day when I would have to come face to face with the reality of my situation. That first day I was going to devote to relaxing and to getting to know Noi again. We spent a long time in bed. Business could wait.

Next day we flew to Cologne to visit my parents. I wanted to explain the situation to them and thank them for guaranteeing my bail. I do not think they really understood exactly what had happened, but they were prepared to accept my assurance that I was an innocent victim. It was good to eat well without worrying how much the bill would come to.

To re-establish myself in business was a matter of getting on the phone to old contacts and spreading the word: the boy is back in town. Sam Evans was re-established in London already and trying to do deals, but this time he was trading in oil rather than weapons. Once bitten, he was not going to try his hand at the arms business again. But I did not share his reluctance. After all, it was what I knew best. I phoned round to see what goods were on offer and tried to spark an interest from somewhere. It was soon apparent that there was plenty of equipment for sale and plenty of potential customers. The trick, as always, was to bring them together.

My initial problem was that I had lost the assured revenue from my advertising agencies. One of the truest maxims in business is that to make money you need money, and that is especially the case if you are trying to do arms deals. You have to be able to afford the considerable expense of actually doing the business. A lot depends on your image – the way you are dressed, the clubs you belong to, the house you live in and your overall lifestyle. If the boys in Victoria Street say 'Come to Iran' and I reply 'You buy my ticket,' then I lose my image. As an international arms dealer you can't afford that. And nobody is impressed by someone who comes to discuss a million-dollar deal and flies economy class.

You should have a secretary to type letters neatly and to answer the phone: much more businesslike than an answer-

ing machine. You need expensive headed stationery. You
need money to take clients out to lunch. I kept up my
membership of Les Ambassadeurs for a while after I got
back, but dropped it when they became understandably
impatient at my unreliability in paying the bills. There is a
lot of competition in this business and to succeed you need
to have something individual to offer. The single unique
thing about me when I returned from America was that I
had been rolled over by the authorities and spent six and a
half months in prison. That is not what your big-buck
customers are looking for when choosing someone to do
business with.

There is no such thing as a steal in the arms trade. Nothing
works within a week: everything takes time. Of the deals
that start, fewer than ten per cent come to fruition. The
problem starts when you call for the letter of credit, asking
the customer to put his money where his mouth is. That is
when you can tell whether the deal is going to work, or
whether it will be a flop. For me a deal becomes realistic
when I see the colour of the buyer's money. It need only be a
telex from a bank saying that the money is available. Once I
have that, the deal is on. The expensive part is waiting for it.

But one of the exciting things about this business is that a
single phone call can alter everything. You are sitting and
wondering how you are going to pay the gas bill, and the
next thing you know a guy phones with a problem and you
can help him solve it. It depends a lot on contacts, on who
you know, and on flexibility. If the quartermaster of some
Middle East army comes to me and says he wants to buy
20,000 tons of frozen chicken, I have to offer it to him.
That's what this whole game is about. I have low overheads
and can make money on small deals.

A lot of people make a big mistake. They look for the
$100 million quick kill. Their percentage is $10 million and
they are made. But if these happen once every five years
they are very lucky. I look for medium-range deals that are
feasible and realistic.

Within a few weeks of my return I was back in the familiar
world of nods and winks and tantalising possibilities. I met a

German who was flying the following day to Riyadh to survey the market, to find out what the military were in need of. If they wanted half a million pairs of socks I could have supplied them. I offer low prices and I have connections with manufacturers in the Far East. On the other hand, if they wanted missiles I could get those too.

I heard that the Iranians were interested in a factory to let them service their tanks themselves and give them new engines, rather than having to rely on getting them from people like the Israelis. Even if the war with Iraq ends tomorrow they will still need the equipment because they will have to build up their forces again. The deal would be worth $10 million, of which my company will make about $1 million. Then I heard about some SAM missiles from the eastern bloc and I offered those to the Iranians – but that market is not so easy for me since I returned from America. The boys at Victoria Street were not so friendly. I was not sorry when the British government sent them packing.

I also ferreted out a Nigerian oil deal. A friend was being offered 200,000 barrels of Bonny Light oil in exchange for arms but he knew nothing about the oil market. I made it my business to find out about it: we would offer it at $5 below the spot-market rate and split the profit.

A company wrote to me about a new product they have developed, a laser rangefinder cheaper and better than any on the market at present. People do not really know how to sell these things. I am working out a project to sell it in the Middle East and South America. The only way to do that is by taking the product in your hands and flying to Abu Dhabi, Dubai, Oman and Saudi Arabia. I arrange appointments for the manufacturers to go and introduce their products to the heads of the army. They do trials and if they are successful we have a deal on our hands. Naturally, I get my cut.

A few weeks after my return to London, I made a list of products available for sale, a kind of Grand Reopening Special Offer catalogue to mark my return to the scene. Here it is:

1. Products available for quick delivery – FOB Europe

Description	Quantity	Price per unit
Sidewinders	200	$33,000
122mm rockets	100,000	$1450
SAM 2	10	$320,000
ZU4 self-propel	6	$1.3m
AK–MS rifles (Poland)	5000	$176
AK 47	5000	$176
Ammo for above	10,000,000	$115 per 1000
60mm mortar rounds	10,000	$30
SAM 7	800	$26,500
Launchers for SAM 7	200	$5500
Launchers for RPG 7	1500	$1670
Hollow charge AT rocket RPG 7	50,000	$158
Ammo 130mm DOR M/46 (1985) (HE and phosphor fuse B427 or AU–18–P1)	100,000	$285
Ammo 122m (1985) HE–M59	18,000 (stock) 100,000 (3-month del.)	$280
Gun complete 130mm M/46	100	$185,000
122mm rocket launcher (self-prop.)	100	$185,000

2. Products from Israel

Description	Quantity	Required by
Battlefield Drohns (plus guarantee of continuous supply of parts)	10	India
F5 planes	25	Brazil
TOWs	100	South Africa
Launchers	20	"
Stinger	100	"
Launchers	20	"
RBS 70	100	"
Launchers	20	"
Mosberg shotgun 8-shot	200 mult.	"

By the time you read this I might have sold none of that material; or I might have made just one sale and put myself back on the road to the big time. Of course it is possible that Uncle Sam might step in and try to ruin my business again by inviting me back to New York to stand trial. During the summer of 1987 the judge dismissed all those charges against us that related to mail and wire fraud, leaving only the charges of conspiring to produce false EUCs. The government are appealing against that decision, which suggests that they plan to go ahead with the trial during 1988.

If they do ask me to return, I am afraid my reply will be: 'Thanks, but no thanks.' They cannot make me go because the offence is not extraditable from Britain. Charlie thinks I should go in any case because there is a good chance of acquittal. I do not plan to put that to the test. It is like what someone said about open-heart surgery: your chance of survival may be good but it's still only 50–50. Of course if I do jump bail it means that I shall never be able to return to the United States for fear of being arrested; but after my single experience of that country, it is a deprivation that I shall be able to bear with equanimity. I shall make my million just the same.

7

What Really Happened

Towards the end of most good crime stories, there occurs a scene where the detective calls all the suspects into a room and proceeds to give a lucid and logical exposition of exactly what happened and who is the guilty party. I wish things were as simple as that in real life, but they seldom are. In trying to untangle a complicated knot you invariably get to a point where whatever strand you work on seems to make the string more tangled, not less.

In my case, in trying to answer the basic question 'Why?' (or more precisely 'Why me?') I face a number of difficulties. I am not a mind-reader and I cannot penetrate the real motives of people working for the US administration. If, after weeks of public hearings and millions of words of reporting, it is still not clear exactly what went on with Oliver North's Irangate deals, how can I, simply a victim, hope to find out what truly lay behind the conspiracy? All I know for certain is its result: I and nine others were deprived of our basic right to liberty by a hostile, scheming government.

The first question is whether the deal that Cyrus Hashemi was trying to bring off ever had any basis in reality, or whether it was never anything more than an imaginary transaction aimed at trapping Sam Evans and the rest of us. I believe very strongly that in the beginning Hashemi was genuinely trying to provide arms for the Iranians, and was only recruited by the customs service after the deal was under way. If that is the case, it seems likely that the deal was originally linked to the arms-for-hostages scenario that North was engaged in, with the approval of the President.

The first and most obvious clue to this lies in Hashemi's record. He had tried to carry off arms-for-hostages deals before, in 1979, just after the fifty-two hostages had been captured in the US embassy in Tehran. So he was a natural person to act as a middleman when the idea came up again.

Hashemi's connection with the American businessman Roy Furmark, a New York energy consultant, provides the first tangible link with the Irangate scenario as we know it. It was Furmark who claimed to have introduced Adnan Kashoggi to Manuchehr Ghorbanifar, the central Iranian figure in the North deals (although some say the two were acquainted earlier). In February 1985, Furmark told Sam Evans that he was putting together a joint venture with Hashemi and Kashoggi to trade with Iran in commodities that included arms. He said that arms deals were already being channelled through Israel with the blessing of the US administration and that direct supplies would similarly be approved. The idea was that Kashoggi should finance the deals, as he did later for Ghorbanifar.

In June 1985 Kashoggi and Ghorbanifar met in the company of Sam Evans and Roy Furmark, in Hamburg. After that, Hashemi and Kashoggi went to Israel where, according to some accounts, they met Shimon Peres, the Prime Minister, and discussed arms supplies. I believe they also met the head of Israeli Military Industries, the organisation that exports arms from Israel. The fact that the Israelis will not confirm either meeting does not mean that they did not take place.

During that month an event occurred that again appears to link Hashemi directly with the arms-for-hostages deals. William Casey, the Director of the Central Intelligence Agency, reported a communication he had received from John Shaheen, an old friend. Shaheen had heard that Hashemi was claiming to have had discussions with the Iranian Foreign Ministry about exchanging American hostages in Beirut for TOW missiles. There would be two other elements of the deal: the United States would have to ensure the release of a group of prisoners in Kuwait that the Iranians had long wanted to have freed; and Hashemi himself would have to be cleared of the outstanding charges against him in New York. The difference between 1985 and 1979 was that this time Hashemi had a strong personal motive to do business, apart from the normal financial spur.

This exchange of messages between Hashemi and Shaheen is mentioned in the report of the Tower Commission – indeed it is the only instance where Hashemi's name appears in the report. There is nothing to show whether this initiative was ever followed through by Casey or any other American official: but if taken at face value it shows that Hashemi may have been in a position to exert influence over the Iranian authorities. It also provides evidence of his strong desire to have the charges against him lifted so that he could travel freely to the United States, and the lengths to which he was prepared to go to ensure this. (Ironically, he did not live to see the charges dropped formally, although he was given generous bail and was not harassed while in the United States.)

Later that summer the partnership between Kashoggi, Hashemi and Furmark was dissolved, apparently because Kashoggi was going through a difficult period financially and was unable to raise the money to guarantee the transactions as he later did for North and Ghorbanifar. Hashemi was still keen to pursue the deals and briefly discussed the possibility of going into partnership with his brother Mohammed Ali (Jamshid), despite an earlier quarrel between them. But that idea came to nothing and he asked Sam to help him set up their operation, offering him 10 per cent of the profits instead of the flat fee that lawyers usually receive.

There can be little doubt that at that time Hashemi was genuinely attempting to arrange arms sales to Iran. It is impossible to be certain exactly when or why he dropped that plan and agreed to co-operate in the US customs sting operation to trap Sam and the rest of us. But it must have been before the meeting at the Raphael Hotel in Paris on 3 December 1985, where Hashemi and Sam met Veillot, Nicos Minardos and some of the other potential suppliers. For it emerged in the court papers that at this meeting Hashemi was wearing a miniature tape recorder underneath his jacket. (It did not in fact work properly and very little of the meeting was recorded – but the thought was there.)

Between September and December Sam had brought Minardos, Veillot and de la Rocque into the deal and introduced them to Hashemi. By October, when Sam first discussed the question with me, Veillot and de la Rocque had already mentioned to Hashemi that they knew how to lay their hands on thirty-nine new F–4E fighter bombers, in their crates in the United States, ready for delivery.

These thirty-nine F–4Es – which nobody, as far as I know, has yet clapped eyes on – are central to solving the mystery. During the Tower Commission's hearings it emerged that they had been discussed with several potential buyers over the previous two years and had even appeared on pro-forma invoices.

In December 1983 Colonel Ralph Broman, who worked for the US Defense Department in Paris, and Paul Cutter, an American diplomat, established European Defense Associates (EDA) to sell arms to Iran as part of an operation called the Demavand project that had been set up with the knowledge of other senior American officials. Bernard Veillot, who appeared to have good connections with the CIA, was introduced to Broman by a State Department official. The F–4Es first surfaced as part of a billion-dollar package offered to Iran by EDA. Among the Iranian representatives at negotiations on this deal was Manuchehr Ghorbanifar.

In February 1985 Veillot signed a contract to supply the planes to the Israeli air force. The contract was drawn up using the headed stationery of a respectable French bank. But the aircraft were obviously never delivered because Veillot threw them into the proposed deal with Hashemi.

The second-hand price of a single F–4E is some $15 million, so thirty-nine of them would come to nearly $600 million – more if they are charged as new. This was a far higher sum, I am sure, than Sam and Hashemi had in mind when they established their company (though not as high as the $2800 million that was the final total of all the offers made). The fact that the planes were to be delivered straight from the United States, apparently without going through an intermediary, added an extra element of risk, especially since Hashemi was under indictment already.

This may have been one of the factors that caused Hashemi to reconsider his role in the affair. Another could have been the difficulty of raising the money. Now that he had parted company with Kashoggi, he had lost his prospective source of finance. So the F–4E deal was beginning to look both too dangerous and too big.

Like the rest of us, Hashemi was aware of the persistent signals from Washington that such deals *were* being made and approved, and he was sure that was the case. But what he did not know for certain was whether *all* deals with Iran were being given official blessing, or only those contracted by people close to the White House. Like everyone else, he had heard President Reagan's speeches denouncing terrorism and his appeals to America's allies to place an embargo on arms to Iran. He knew about Operation Staunch.

So the signals coming from Washington, although confirming that arms sales were being sanctioned, were confused as to the extent of the approval. As a regular gambler in the West End casinos, with a reputation for cunning, Hashemi knew how to calculate odds. He thought he might be able to improve his chance of winning by switching his bet before the ball was thrown into the roulette wheel – or, better still, by coming to an arrangement with the croupier.

So he asked his New York lawyer to make discreet inquiries at the District Attorney's office on two distinct aspects of the matter. The answers were: no, it was not official policy to sanction arms deals with Iran; and yes, they would be happy to come to an arrangement about the outstanding charges against Hashemi, provided he was prepared to do them a little favour. That, I believe, was where the sting began. The half-billion dollars on deposit at the Chemical Bank never existed – and seeing that Sam told me about the money when we spoke in October 1985, the operation must have been under way by then.

With Hashemi dead, it will never be possible to discover with any certainty why he acted as he did, sacrificing the liberty of seventeen men, including some like Sam who had thought of themselves as his friends, in order to be rid of a legal case that cannot have been more than a minor inconvenience. Being barred from returning to the United States must have been galling for him but it represented only a small restriction in his lifestyle: he could have lived a perfectly fulfilling and profitable existence in the fleshpots of Europe. But the Middle Eastern mind is hard to fathom. As I remarked in an earlier chapter, it is not in the Islamic nature to forge reliable friendships with outsiders. Considerations of personal self-interest and survival are what motivate them.

And I suppose in Hashemi's case there could have been a second motive. Ever since the Americans first imposed their embargo in 1979, Iranian representatives have had to dash around the world making furtive, undignified deals with suspect people in the arms trade. They gained the reputation of being a soft touch, willing to pay stratospheric prices for the goods – and, when they had done so, sometimes not receiving them. Inevitably, they were regularly taken for a ride by unscrupulous dealers. Hashemi, who had been an arms dealer for some years, had probably suffered in that way himself.

When the offer of the thirty-nine F–4Es was made, he may have thought it so outlandish that it could only be another attempt at a rip-off. And even if it was not, it presented an obvious opportunity to gain revenge for the swindles perpetrated on him and his fellow Iranians in the past. It is not hard to see how he could have persuaded himself that to co-operate in the sting was a matter of honour for himself and his country.

Did North know what Hashemi and the US customs were up to? Because there are so many back-links between characters in the Hashemi deal and the Irangate deals, it is almost inconceivable that he did not. There is no evidence that he did anything to stop the sting operation, so it is likely that he approved of it. One theory is that he masterminded it, in order to leave the field clear for his own Iran deals and the profits they made for the Contras.

There is one further fascinating link. On the day we were all rounded up in New York and Bermuda, Ghorbanifar, on a visit to Switzerland, was arrested there, presumably at the request of the US government. He spent a day in prison until he was released, probably again with American approval. This incident, mentioned in *The Chronology*, may have been meant as a warning shot across Ghorbanifar's bows, reminding him that the only safe channel for pursuing the arms deals was North and the National Security Council.

If the extent and nature of the US government's involvement in our case is hard to fathom, that of the Israeli government is even harder. Israel is not an open society in the sense that America is: there have been no Tower Commissions or Congressional hearings there. I was not involved in the Israeli deal but Sam is adamant that he met Israeli officials on his visit to Jerusalem in the summer of 1985 and was certain that they were giving the go-ahead for the transaction. In one of his taped conversations with Hashemi, Sam said, 'I am told that this is right through to Peres and Rabin, and they are all watching this deal very, very, very closely. . . . You have the full and complete co-operation of the authorities. . . . I've met with the [Israeli] Ministry of Defence people who make it quite clear that they definitely approve of this deal, no question about it.' And as Nicos said in another recorded conversation, the Israelis would be unlikely to do anything of that sort without at least tacit encouragement from Washington.

On the face of it, the participation of General Bar-Am, a hero of the Middle East wars of 1967 and 1973, suggests approval at a high level, but it is not conclusive. He is one of some 800 former Israeli military personnel who carry letters from their government authorising them to look for markets for Israeli arms, although not to engage in negotiations on behalf of the Defence Ministry. He was Chief of Staff of the manpower branch of the Israeli Defence Forces until made to resign in 1984 in a minor scandal in which there were questions about his practices with regard to promotions, and it was suggested he had handed out weapons to personal friends.

Israeli spokesmen have denied any involvement by their government, but this means little because such denials are routine: they insisted they knew nothing about the Irangate transactions until conclusive proof was produced by the Tower Commission.

In any event, the Israelis have made no secret about their willingness to facilitate the supply of arms to Iran. The Americans have customarily turned a blind eye. In 1984 Ariel Sharon, the former Defence Minister, gave a speech in Connecticut in which he admitted as much, pointing to the danger of Soviet penetration of the Middle East if Iraq won the war. Efraim Poran, a former military adviser to Prime Minister Shamir, was quoted in the *Los Angeles Times* as saying about this case, 'There is a rule that the enemy of your enemy is your friend. So basically, for Israel I think Iran is doing, if I may say so, a positive job.'

Poran said it would have been impossible for so many weapons to leave Israel without the government knowing. Officially there was an understanding with Washington that American arms would not be re-exported to Iran but the Americans were not interested in enforcing it rigidly: it was easy to breach it while going through the motions of complying. An end-user certificate could be bought from the Philippines (when Marcos was President) or Turkey for $100,000. Poran explained: 'With this paper you go to the United States, you buy the things, you put them on a ship and in the middle of the ocean you change the papers of the ship and she goes instead to Iran or any other country and you make the deal. This is the way that things are done.' He added that in his experience it was generally done with the connivance of the Israeli government. And this was confirmed by an unnamed Pentagon official who told the New York newspaper *Newsday*, 'No one who is a serious student of Israel would believe for a moment that Israelis would be able to acquire Israeli-origin equipment and sell it on the black or grey market without the knowledge of Israeli officials.'

Whatever the Israeli level of complicity at *government* level in the Hashemi affair, there can scarcely be any doubt that Mossad, their intelligence service, knew what was going on and played a role. In one of the taped meetings, Sam Evans said that Mossad told him that they had asked the American Central Intelligence Agency to put a 'tracer' on him so that they could judge whether he was reliable. Mossad's part in this was confirmed by the Israeli defendants.

It was Mossad that warned Evans and the Israeli group that they must persuade Hashemi to meet them in Bermuda rather than anywhere in the United States. This was not, apparently, because they knew the group would be arrested in New York, but they believed there was a danger of news of the deal leaking out if they were all there at the same time. This would have embarrassed both Israel and the United States.

Bar-Am claimed that, on the day after his arrest in Bermuda, Mossad agents ran a check on the US customs investigators in charge of the case – although he did not reveal how he came by this information. His first phone call after his arrest was to the Israeli military attaché in Washington. Press reports said that he threatened to blow the whistle on government involvement in the deal unless the Israelis intervened on his behalf; but he was told that he was on his own.

(Bar-Am never carried out that threat. He was distinctly uncommunicative during the short time he was on our floor at the MCC, and has offered no further revelations beyond what he had said as an immediate, petulant response to his arrest.)

I believe that Veillot and de la Rocque had connections with the CIA – which was how they came to have such sound information about what was going on. De la Rocque was certainly linked with one of the many mystery figures in the case, Richard Brenneke, a businessman from Oregon who worked for the CIA for thirteen years. In the first of a series of memos about arms sales to Iran that he wrote to people in the administration from November 1985 onwards, Brenneke described de la Rocque as his associate. On 1 January 1986 he wrote a further memo to the Pentagon revealing the proposed deal with Hashemi and his Galaxy Trade Incorporated, and even quoting the number of the account at the Chemical Bank where the Iranian money was supposed to have been deposited.

Presumably he had obtained this information from de la Rocque. But an even more intriguing aspect of Brenneke's role is that only three days later he wrote another memo, this time to the State Department, outlining Iran's terms for swapping hostages for arms supplies. This again suggests a link between the Hashemi deal and the hostage swap. Brenneke was surprised about how little interest was shown by anyone in Washington at his disclosures, and wrote to Vice-President Bush to this effect on 15 January. The reason for the lack of interest, of course, was that the people who needed to know already knew. (Brenneke was only able to arrange a meeting at the Pentagon at the end of May – a month after our arrest.)

In trying to pin down what anyone in the US administration or the CIA knew, the greatest difficulty is in guessing how much the different levels and departments of government co-operate and exchange information. At the hearings by the Tower Commission and the Congressional committees, the questioning constantly came back to that point, and the answers were seldom consistent. It was never possible to get a precise picture of what anyone was being told, from the President down. Even when an official had initialled documents, supposedly showing that he had read or approved them, questions were raised as to whether he had merely signed routinely (even inadvertently), without being at all sure what the documents were about.

We were told, for instance, that George Shultz had known nothing about Colonel North's arms sales to Iran: then the story was that he *had* known but had not approved. William Casey seems to have known what was going on most of the time, but did that necessarily mean that the information filtered down to other employees of the CIA? Conversely, even if some people in the CIA had learned from Mossad about the deals Sam Evans was trying to make with

Hashemi, did that mean that Casey himself had been told? I think even Agatha Christie would find it hard to work out a sensible solution to a mystery with so many unknown and variable factors.

The greatest puzzle of all is the death in July 1986 of Cyrus Hashemi. I have already gone into this in some detail but let me recap the facts that persuaded those closest to him that he might have been murdered. Essentially, there are two puzzles: first, the sudden diagnosis of a fatal illness in a man who had been in perfect health and had received a favourable medical check-up only a month earlier; and secondly the unhelpful attitude of the authorities on the matter of the autopsy. Mohammed Ali Hashemi, his brother, has been thwarted whenever he has tried to get more information. He was told, for instance, that some of the X-ray pictures taken of Hashemi before he died had unaccountably disappeared from the Cromwell Hospital: but the doctor in charge of his case, Dr James Sharp, will not confirm or deny that story.

If Hashemi *was* killed, who by? Houshang Lavi says he was told by Joe King that 'we', presumably the US customs, had to 'get rid of him' because he knew too much. That might be true: it would fit in with the philosophy of the American security services that human lives are expendable if the national interests are at stake. But knowing Joe King, he could just as easily be inventing the story to burnish his ruthless image. (As indeed could Lavi, who is something of a showman.)

Although Charlie Theofan thinks Hashemi's death makes our case harder to defend, it cannot make the prosecution's task that much easier – at least not so much as to justify having him killed. There had been talk that he was angry because the charges against him had not been formally dropped as he had been promised. The District Attorney could have been waiting until he had secured our conviction before fulfilling his side of the bargain to the letter, and maybe the star witness had retaliated by growing uncooperative and threatening not to play his allotted role in court. That would have been a setback for the prosecution but surely not grounds for murder. And even if it seems certain that the prosecution are trying to deter any investigation into the death, that does not in itself prove that they were responsible for it. They might calculate that an investigation, whatever its outcome, could prove embarrassing simply for the facts it uncovers about Hashemi and the sting operation.

Looking elsewhere for possible culprits, it is not out of the question that someone in the large and secretive network of Iran's arms merchants might have had a score to settle with Hashemi. After all, he co-operated with the Americans – who are highly unpopular in Iran – in a trap directed against people seeking to provide the country with weapons to pursue its 'patriotic' war with Iraq. We, the victims of the sting, were no doubt doing it primarily to make a profit, but in practical terms we were helping Iran. So what Hashemi did to us was not likely to make him popular with his compatriots.

The Israelis, too, could have wanted Hashemi out of the way. Clearly embarrassed by General Bar-Am's role in the affair, they might have thought that the Iranian knew too much about their involvement. To me, though, this seems the least likely explanation. If it were true, it would mean that a lot of other people connected with the case would have had to be silenced before Israel's secrets could be regarded as secure.

So several motives existed. What about the means? Dr Sharp is adamant that death was caused by acute leukaemia. Stories of the existence of a drug that duplicates symptoms of that disease may sound far-fetched, but when security services are involved almost anything is possible. I remember a case in London a few years ago when a Bulgarian émigré who worked for the BBC was killed after being pricked by the poisoned tip of an umbrella at a bus stop. That sounded like spy fiction, but it was true.

Hashemi's brother Mohammed Ali is still trying to get to the bottom of his death. If the mystery were ever solved it would help clear up the other puzzles in this affair.

*

Although that might never happen, I have no doubt about who is the guilty party in my own case. I put the entire blame on the government of the United States. Just because it is the largest country in the world, it thinks it can run everything to its own liking. It talks about opposing terrorism and backs guerrilla movements against legitimate governments – like in Nicaragua and, a few years ago, Grenada. What gives it the right?

But for a country that sometimes seems to want to run the world, I should have thought that the most important priority was to decide who runs the country. Who does run America? It cannot be the President because, if we are to believe him, he is not always told what is going on. The Congress, representing the people, knows even less, at least until it is much too late.

And then, who runs the law-enforcement departments? Does something with such important policy implications as a sting, an attempt to trap innocent people – does that have to be approved by the Attorney-General? Or can individual district attorneys do it on their own responsibility?

Who controls the CIA and the NSC? Can their agents do what they like without referring it higher? And would that include having people killed, as they may have done in the case of Hashemi? Until those questions are answered satisfactorily, we have to assume that anarchy prevails at the highest levels of government in the areas of foreign policy and the administration of justice.

I do not pretend that I am a philanthropist – I am in the arms business for money – but I have no guilt about trying to sell countries weapons to defend themselves. Iran, like any other nation, has the right to do that. I sell the tools of self-defence and security.

In an absolutely fair legal system, I could never be found guilty. How can you be convicted of doing something authorised by the government? But then in an absolutely fair system I should not have been held in America against my will for ten and a half months.

As I write, it is still not certain whether our case will ever come to trial. A lot hinges on what (if any) charges are laid against Oliver North by the special prosecutor appointed to look into the Irangate affair. If there *is* a trial of our case, however the verdict goes, I know in my heart that I am not guilty.

Appendix 1

Chronology

(Dates in bold type refer to my own experiences.)

1979

16 January: Shah of Iran overthrown by supporters of Ayatollah Khomeini.

4 November: US Embassy personnel seized by Iranians and held hostage. President Carter imposes an embargo on trade with Iran.

7 December: Cyrus Hashemi proposes to the US administration that Iran might exchange the hostages for arms. The plan apparently did not go forward.

1980

25 April: Daring bid to rescue Iranian hostages by helicopter fails as engines become clogged with dust.

May: I join Mönch, a military publisher in Cologne – my introduction to the arms business.

22 September: Iraqi army crosses Iranian border to begin war. Iraqi aircraft attack Iranian airfields.

4 November: Ronald Reagan defeats Jimmy Carter in US Presidential election, partly because hostage issue still unresolved.

10 November: Iraq captures Khorramshahr and controls 4000 square miles of Iranian territory.

1981

20 January: On the day of President Reagan's inauguration, the hostages are released after 444 days. As part of the agreement, US lifts many of the trade sanctions against

Iran but the arms embargo is maintained.

28 September: Iraqi siege of Abadan, important Iranian oil centre, is defeated.

14 December: Israel annexes Golan Heights from Syria. US cancels 'memorandum of understanding' with Israel signed two weeks earlier.

1982

21 May: Newspaper columnists Evans and Novak report that Israel has been secretly shipping arms to Iran. The US administration knows but has done nothing to prevent it, they say.

24 May: Iran recaptures Khorramshahr.

13 July: Iranian forces cross into Iraqi territory for first time, moving towards Basra.

July: Iranian troops at the port of Bandar Abbas refuse to allow a Danish ship to unload a consignment of grenades because crates are marked 'Made in USA'.

18 August: Israeli government confirm they have been selling Iran spare parts for aircraft.

29 September: Ian Smalley, a British arms dealer based in Texas, is indicted for conspiring to sell tanks and TOW missiles to Iran, as a result of a government sting operation.

September: I go to London and arrange to join Jane's, the British military publishers, the following year. On this trip I meet Noi.

November: Israel reported to be selling TOW missiles to Iran.

December: I leave Monch. Noi comes to Cologne for Christmas and we return to London together on 26 December.

1983

16 February: Ian Smalley (see 29/9/82) acquitted because jury do not believe key prosecution witness.

March: I take work as a truck driver while waiting to start at Jane's.

April: US administration launch Operation Staunch to deter allies from selling arms to Iran.

April: Iraqis begin missile attacks on Iranian towns.

June: I start work with Jane's.

25 July: Time magazine reports that hundreds of millions of dollars worth of American equipment is being sold to Iran and names Cyrus Hashemi and his brother Balanian as two of the main dealers for the Iranians, through a London company called Zoomer Fly Ltd.

23 October: The US Marine compound at Beirut airport is bombed by terrorists and 241 servicemen are killed. The US says it has evidence implicating Iran in the outrage.

December: My first independent deal for military equipment: army boots for Saudi Arabia.

1984

January: Returning from a trip to Vienna I sit next to John Saunders, who later becomes my partner.

20 January: George Shultz, US Secretary of State, officially declares Iran to be a sponsor of international terrorism.

16 March: William Buckley, CIA station chief in Beirut, is kidnapped by terrorists.

27 March: Iraqis extend war with Iran by attacking tankers in the Gulf.

May: John and I establish International Services Bellfine Ltd and International Procurement and Sales. I leave Jane's but continue to work for them on commission. I make my first visit to the Iranian arms-procurement office in Victoria Street.

June: I go to Abu Dhabi, Dubai and Oman to prospect for business.

July: My first deal in military hardware: machine guns for Chile.

October: US intelligence study discusses possibility of restoring diplomatic relations with Iran and resuming arms sales.

November: I am introduced to Sam Evans by Robert Mills of Les Ambassadeurs.

19 November: Hamburg meeting between Iranian middle-man Manuchehr Ghorbanifar and Theodore Shackley, former CIA officer. Discussions include resumption of normal relations between US and Iran, arms supplies and the release of US hostages in Beirut.

3 December: Peter Kilburn, librarian at American University in Beirut, is kidnapped there – the first of ten westerners held in the space of six months.

1985

January: William Casey, Director of the CIA, tells American businessman Roy Furmark that arms deals with Iran are being approved by US administration. Furmark meets Ghorbanifar and Saudi arms dealer Adnan Kashoggi to discuss arms-for-hostages swap.

February: Furmark tells Sam Evans, his lawyer, that he plans to set up a company with Cyrus Hashemi and Kashoggi to sell commodities to Iran, including arms.

27 February: French dealer Bernard Veillot signs contract to supply thirty-nine F–4E jet fighters to Iranian air force.

April: Michael Ledeen, a consultant to the National Security Commission, visits Israel to discuss possible Israeli assistance in an arms-for-hostages deal.

May: Furmark and Kashoggi meet Ghorbanifar in Hamburg to discuss arms sales to Iran.

17 May: CIA document recommends easing of global restrictions on arms sales to Iran. Caspar Weinberger, Secretary for Defense, is against it.

June: William Buckley dies in the custody of Islamic Jihad but his death is not revealed until October.

13 June: Another Hamburg meeting between Furmark, Kashoggi and Ghorbanifar, this time involving Sam Evans as well.

14 June: Two Lebanese men hijack a TWA aircraft between Athens and Rome and force it to fly to Beirut. One American passenger killed and thirteen taken prisoner in Beirut.

30 June: The thirteen hostages released, apparently after

secret discussions between American and Iranian officials
and intervention by Hashemi Rafsanjani, Speaker of the
Iranian Parliament.

3 July: David Kimche, Director-General of the Israeli
Foreign Ministry, has talks with Robert McFarlane, the
President's National Security Adviser, in Washington.
Kimche says that Iran is interested in opening political
contacts with the United States. A few days later
McFarlane reports this to the President and other
officials. During numerous conversations this month
involving Israelis, Iranians and Americans, specific proposals are drawn up for exchanging arms for the release of
hostages.

8 July: President Reagan, in a speech to the American Bar
Association, accuses Iran of being responsible for international terrorism and says America will never make
concessions to terrorists.

August: William von Raab, US Customs Commissioner,
says that Cyrus Hashemi is on the list of the ten most
wanted arms dealers.

6 August: President Reagan gives oral approval for the
supply of American arms to Iran via Israel.

30 August: A shipment of American arms, including 100
TOW missiles, leaves Israel en route to Iran. Finance
arranged by Adnan Kashoggi who has reportedly borrowed some of the money from 'Tiny' Rowland.

13 September: Another 408 TOW missiles sent from Israel to
Iran.

15 September: One American hostage, the Rev. Benjamin
Weir, is released. The Americans believe that this is a
direct result of the arms supplies and that more hostages
will be released shortly.

October 1985: Sam Evans tells me about the Hashemi deal
and asks me to quote for equipment. I tell him about the
fifteen F–4E fighters that the Egyptian air force want to
dispose of.

7 October: The Italian cruise ship *Achille Lauro* is hijacked
by Palestinian terrorists. One American passenger is
killed.

10 October: Colonel Oliver North helps arrange the interception of an Egyptian plane carrying the hijackers, which is forced down in Sicily.

November: Cyrus Hashemi does a deal with US customs that he will not be prosecuted if he agrees to take part in a sting operation.

14 November: Colonel North meets Terry Waite, the Archbishop of Canterbury's envoy, in London.

23 November: Eighteen of a planned shipment of eighty American HAWK missiles are transported to Iran. No US hostages are released and next February most of the missiles are returned as being unsuitable for Iran's purposes.

30 November: Businessman Richard Brenneke, an associate of John de la Rocque, writes the first of a number of memos to Vice-President Bush and other officials about private attempts to sell arms to Iran.

December: After an approach by an Israeli in London, I fly to Zurich to meet Sam Hecht, an Israeli arms dealer, who is also interested in buying the Egyptian F–4Es for Iran.

3 December: Hashemi, Evans, Veillot and de la Rocque meet at the Raphael Hotel in Paris. Hashemi wears a secret microphone.

4 December: President Reagan announces resignation of Robert McFarlane, effective in January, and his replacement as National Security Adviser by Vice-Admiral John Poindexter.

5 December: According to Poindexter (at 1987 Congressional hearings), President Reagan signs a secret document authorising sale of US arms to Iran.

9 December: First taped telephone call between Evans and Hashemi.

27 December: Bomb explosions at Rome and Vienna airports kill twenty people.

31 December: In a recorded phone conversation, Bernard Veillot tells Hashemi that Vice-President Bush is about to give US approval to their arms deal.

1986

1 January: In a further memo, Brenneke asserts that Poindexter has given approval for the sale of 10,000 TOW missiles to Iran.

6 January: President Reagan signs a Finding authorising shipment of American arms from Israel to Iran.

7 January: Another meeting at the Raphael, this time attended by two customs agents posing as advisers to Hashemi. Veillot says the proposed deal is about to get the approval of Vice-President Bush.

11 January: Veillot tells Sam and Hashemi that he may now only be able to get his hands on up to thirteen of the thirty-nine F–4Es originally promised. He talks of the possibility of getting an end-user certificate from Latin America.

14 January: I prepare an invoice for Hashemi for fifteen F–4Es, plus spare parts and shipping costs, totally $253.6 million.

17 January: President Reagan signs a further Finding, this time authorising arms sales to Iran directly from the United States.

5 February: Meeting between Iranian and American delegations in Frankfurt, attended by North and Ghorbanifar.

6 February: Hashemi calls me again re proof of funds. With problem unresolved we have no further contact until April.

7 February: Sam Evans tells Hashemi that Washington has given the green light for the deal, despite George Shultz being against it. He says Vice-President Bush is in favour.

13 February: 1000 TOW missiles sent from US to Israel en route for Iran as part of the North hostage deal.

24 February: Another Frankfurt meeting between Iranian and US officials.

26 February: Sam Evans goes to New York to meet Hashemi.

8 March: North and Ghorbanifar meet in Paris, but hoped-for release of hostages does not take place.

10 March: Evans and Nicos Minardos go to Jerusalem to see the Eisenbergs and Israeli officials.

April: 'Tiny' Rowland, chief executive of Lonrho, is approached by Kashoggi to help finance some of the North/Ghorbanifar deals. Told they are authorised by the US government, he checks with Charles Price, US Ambassador in London.

13 April: Sam Evans and the Israeli group dealing with Hashemi meet to finalise details of their deal.

14 April: I go to Marbella to pursue sale of Milan missiles to Iran.

15 April: US jets bomb Libya as punishment for alleged Libyan involvement in an explosion in a Berlin discotheque earlier in the month. In retaliation Peter Kilburn, one of the US hostages in Beirut, is killed.

17 April: Returning from Spain I receive my first call from Hashemi for more than two months. He asks me to go as soon as possible to New York, where I will receive a down-payment for one amplifier. If the deal is not made in a few days, he says, funds will be repatriated to Iran.

21 April: I fly to New York, meet Hashemi and am then arrested by US customs. Charged with mail fraud, wire fraud and conspiracy to breach Iranian arms embargo and obtain false EUCs. Four other defendants arrested separately in New York.

22 April: Sam Evans and the Israeli group detained in Bermuda. William von Raab, US Customs Commissioner, describes the defendants as 'brokers of death'.

23 May: Robert McFarlane, former National Security Adviser to the President, flies to Tehran with North and others in a plane carrying spare parts for HAWK missiles. He has talks with Iranian officials, but no hostages are released.

29 May: Sam Evans and the Israeli group join the rest of us at the Metropolitan Correction Center.

June: Sam Evans released on bail of $4½ million. Over the next few weeks, other defendants are released as bail money is raised.

21 July: Cyrus Hashemi dies in London. Autopsy gives cause of death as acute myeloblastic leukaemia.

26 July: Rev. Lawrence Jenco, former head of Catholic

relief services in Beirut, is released after eighteen months in captivity. North and Poindexter claim this is a direct result of the McFarlane trip in May.

3 August: Spare parts for HAWK missiles delivered from Israel to Iran.

7 October: Roy Furmark visits William Casey at Kashoggi's request to say that Kashoggi is finding it hard to extract payment from the Iranians for the arms deliveries.

29 October: New consignment of 500 TOW missiles sent from Israel to Iran. Understanding is that three US hostages will be released.

30 October: I am freed from prison on bail of $52,500. I stay in Westport, Connecticut. I plan escape from USA.

2 November: Only one hostage, David Jacobsen, is released following latest weapons delivery.

3 November: First press report in Beirut of McFarlane trip to Tehran and North's supplies of US arms to Iran.

5 November: Arms-for-hostages story reaches US papers and is dubbed 'Irangate'.

13 November: President Reagan admits on television that 'small amounts of defensive weapons and spare parts' have gone to Iran from USA.

17 November: Lorna Schofield, the prosecutor, says that despite Irangate the case against us will go ahead.

21 November: As danger grows of more details of the Iran transactions being revealed, North and his secretary Fawn Hall shred documents in his office.

25 November: Diversion of profits from Iranian arms sales to help Contra rebels in Nicaragua is revealed. Admiral Poindexter resigns as President's National Security Adviser and North is dismissed from NSC. Israel admits its role in the supply of arms to Iran.

26 November: Tower Commission appointed to look into Iran/Contra affair.

10 December: Robert Vining, a US district judge, recommends immediate release of Lemuel Stevens, a man he sentenced to imprisonment in Dallas in 1985 for arms dealing with Iran. Vining argues that the US government has been shown to have done the same thing.

15 December: William Casey, Director of the CIA, admitted to hospital with brain cancer, the day before he is due to testify before the Senate Intelligence Committee.

19 December: Lawrence Walsh is appointed independent counsel to prosecute cases arising from Iran/Contra affair, but he declines to take over the prosecution of our case.

1987

12 January: Terry Waite, the Archbishop of Canterbury's envoy, flies to Beirut to negotiate the release of hostages but is himself kidnapped.

2 February: William Casey resigns as Director of the CIA.

9 February: Robert McFarlane takes an overdose of Valium in an apparent suicide attempt, on the eve of a scheduled appearance before the Tower Commission.

18 February: I am finally given my passport back and allowed to return to London.

27 February: Donald Regan, President Reagan's chief of staff, resigns and is replaced by Howard Baker.

14 March: President Reagan, in a radio talk, says he should have taken heed of the warnings given by Shultz and Weinberger against approving arms sales to Iran.

May: Congressional hearings on Iran/Contra dealings begin. William Casey dies of cancer.

7 July: Colonel North begins testimony at Congressional hearings in Washington.

25 July: Poindexter tells Congressional hearing that 'our policy was not an arms embargo against Iran'.

August: Judge Sand dismisses all charges against defendants relating to mail and wire fraud, leaving only four charges of conspiracy to obtain false EUCs. Prosecution appeals against decision. Our trial postponed to January 1988 at the earliest.

Appendix 2

The Charges

This is a verbatim transcript of the sections of the indictment relevant to me from *United States of America v. Evans et al* (United States District Court, Southern District of New York).

The Grand Jury further charges:

14. From on or about December 23, 1985, up to and including April 21, 1986, in the Southern District of New York and elsewhere, the defendants SAMUEL EVANS, HERMANN MOLL and INTERNATIONAL PROCUREMENT AND SALES, INC. (hereafter 'INTERNATIONAL PROCUREMENT'), together with others unknown to the Grand Jury, unlawfully, wilfully and knowingly did combine, conspire, confederate and agree together and with each other:

a. to defraud the United States and its agencies, the Department of State and the Department of Defense, of their right to conduct their affairs free from fraud, false statements, chicanery and deceit, to wit, the right of the State Department and Defense Department, delegated by the President of the United States, to regulate and control the exportation and subsequent resale and transfer of U.S. Defense Articles in accordance with the foreign policy of the United States, as provided in Title 22, United States Code, Sections 2751, 2752, 2753, 2761, 2762 and 2778, and Title 22, Code of Federal Regulations, Subchapter M (International Traffic In Arms Regulations);

b. to violate Title 22, United States Code, Section 2778(c), and Title 22, Code of Federal Regulations, Sections 121.1, 123.9, 123.10, 126.1(a) and 127, by combining, conspiring, confederating and agreeing together and with each other to make an untrue statement of a material fact and omit to state a material fact required to be stated in applications to the United States Department of State or the United States Department of Defense for approval to resell, divert, transfer, transship and dispose of certain U.S. Defense Articles; and

c. to violate Title 18, United States Code, Section 1001, by combining, conspiring, confederating and agreeing together and with each other to falsify, conceal and cover up by trick, scheme and device, a material fact, and to make and cause to be made false, fictitious and fraudulent statements and representations, and use and cause to be used false writings and documents knowing the same to contain false, fictitious and fraudulent statements, in a matter within the jurisdiction of the United States Department of State and the United States Department of Defense, both departments and agencies of the United States.

Object of the Conspiracy

15. An object of the conspiracy was to resell, divert, transfer, transship and dispose of the following U.S. Defense Articles, among others, from a foreign country or countries to and in Iran, contrary to the policy of the United States to prevent the transfer of U.S. Defense Articles to Iran and to deny licenses and other approvals relating to U.S. Defense Articles destined for Iran:

15	F–4 Aircraft
10	Engines for F–4 Aircraft
	Spare Parts for F–4 Aircraft
200	Engines for M–48 Tanks
15	VA–145 Pulsed Twystr. Amplifiers

Methods and Means of the Conspiracy

16. Among the methods and means to be employed by the defendants and their co-conspirators in accomplishing the conspiracy were the following:

A. It was a part of the conspiracy that the defendant SAMUEL EVANS would act as an intermediary between buyer and seller.

B. It was further part of the conspiracy that the defendant HERMANN MOLL, together with others unknown to the Grand Jury, through the defendant INTERNATIONAL PROCUREMENT, would obtain U.S. Defense Articles and sell them to Galaxy Trade Inc. for Iran.

C. It was further part of the conspiracy that the defendant HERMANN MOLL and others unknown to the Grand Jury would obtain end user certificates that would falsely and fraudulently attest that the U.S. Defense Articles were destined for a country acceptable to the United States.

D. It was further part of the conspiracy that the defendants, SAMUEL EVANS and HERMANN MOLL, together with others unknown to the Grand Jury, would represent and cause to be represented to the United States Department of State or Defense in applications to export or to resell, divert, transfer, transship and dispose of the U.S. Defense Articles that they were destined for country or countries that were acceptable to the United States.

OVERT ACTS

17. In furtherance of this conspiracy and to effect its objects, the following overt acts, among others, were committed:

A. On or about December 23, 1985, the defendant SAMUEL EVANS informed the putative buyer of U.S. Defense Articles for Iran of the availability for sale of 15 F–4 Aircraft then held by the Egyptian Air Force, in addition to other items of military hardware.

B. On or about January 14, 1986, and January 17, 1986, the defendant HERMANN MOLL signed pro forma invoices of the defendant INTERNATIONAL PRO-CUREMENT offering U.S. Defense Articles.

C. During the period from on or about January 29, 1986, up to and including February 7, 1986, the defendant

HERMANN MOLL attempted to obtain satisfactory proof of funds available in the Southern District of New York for the purchase of U.S. Defense Articles.

D. On or about February 7, 1986, the defendant SAMUEL EVANS wrote a letter to the defendant HERMANN MOLL assuring the availability of funds.

E. On or about April 21, 1986, in the Southern District of New York, the defendant HERMANN MOLL met with the putative buyer for Iran and discussed the proposed sale described in the foregoing paragraphs.

(Title 18, United States Code, Section 371.)

Index